Erskine Caldwell

Twayne's United States Authors Series

Kenneth Eble, Editor
University of Utah

TUSAS 469

ERSKINE CALDWELL
(1902–   )
Photograph by Margaret Bourke-White
Courtesy of Roger B. White

Erskine Caldwell

By James E. Devlin
State University of New York
College at Oneonta

Twayne Publishers • Boston

Erskine Caldwell

James E. Devlin

Copyright © 1984 by G. K. Hall & Company
All Rights Reserved
Published by Twayne Publishers
A Division of G. K. Hall & Company
70 Lincoln Street
Boston, Massachusetts 02111

Book Production by Marne B. Sultz

Book Design by Barbara Anderson

Printed on permanent/durable acid-free
paper and bound in the United States of
America.

Library of Congress Cataloging in Publication Data

Devlin, James E., 1938–
  Erskine Caldwell.

  (Twayne's United States author series ; TUSAS 469)
  Bibliography: p. 152
  Includes index.
  1. Caldwell, Erskine, 1903–   —Criticism and
interpretation.   I. Title.   II. Series.
PS3505.A322Z56   1984   813'.52   83-26538
ISBN 0-8057-7410-6

Meiner Frau

Contents

About the Author

Born in Boston in 1938, James E. Devlin attended public schools there, graduating from Boston Latin School in 1955. He received a B.S. degree from Boston College and an M.A.T. from Harvard University. After military service and discharge from the 1st Battle Group, First Infantry, at West Point in 1964, he came to the State College at Oneonta, New York, where he is currently Professor of English. In 1976 he received a Ph.D. from the State University of New York at Binghamton and was appointed to a Fulbright lectureship at the Paedagogische Hochschule in Goettingen, West Germany. His publications in various journals reflect an interest chiefly in American literature of the previous century, often where it impinges upon German themes and experiences.

Preface

The enormous success of Jack Kirkland's staging of *Tobacco Road* brought public attention in early 1934 to a young southern writer who had already been noticed by reviewers for two collections of short stories, *American Earth* (1931) and *We Are the Living* (1933), and two novels, *Tobacco Road* (1932) and *God's Little Acre* (1933). Viking Press had just defeated the New York Society for the Suppression of Vice with a well-publicized defense of that last earthy story, and Caldwell, who was temporarily working for Hollywood, gave promise that he could satisfy both popular and critical tastes. Here was a writer out of the Southern Renaissance who wrote taut American English with a distinct social consciousness in the worst years of the Depression, yet whose rich humor demonstrated that comic perception and harsh realism were not mutually exclusive. His ribald stories of grotesque rural Americans baffled by the world about them, narrated with calculated understatement, inspired critics to link his name with Anderson's and Hemingway's and to utter extravagant predictions for his future. But at thirty-two, only three years after his long apprenticeship had ended, Caldwell's most significant books were already behind him. During the next ten years, he published all the remaining fiction that would ever merit serious critical consideration: *Journeyman* (1935), *Trouble in July* (1940), *Georgia Boy* (1943), *Tragic Ground* (1944), and the short story collections, *Kneel to the Rising Sun* (1935), *Southways* (1938), and *Jackpot* (1940).

From 1934 to 1944, Caldwell's star rose to a peak and rapidly declined. Though he has continued to write into the late 1970s, critics had all but abandoned him by the end of World War II. His mass audience followed him well into the 1950s but it too declined, though never to a point where he has not had a half dozen or more titles in print or lacked a publisher. Today, almost fifty years after *Tobacco Road* and *God's Little Acre* and despite the fact that his books have sold millions of copies—from forty to seventy-five million depending on who issues the figures—Caldwell is largely forgotten. His name means nothing to the young, and to older readers it invokes only the memory of an author whose best-selling books were once considered salacious. Academic criticism has neglected him for many years, though he still elicits passing reference in histories of American literature or specialized studies. In these he is inevitably grouped with other writers to whom he is unfavorably compared.

For Eastern Europe he remained till recently a protest writer who exposed the plight of the tenant farmer and the American black. Often, however, he has been classified according to the dominant interest of the critic considering him. Thus, to a Marxist, he is a socialist waging war with a committed pen. To the historical or cultural student of American literature, he is another southern humorist, a local colorist, a naturalist, an observer of the hopelessness of the South where—as a reputable German-American man of letters assured his readers several decades ago—alcohol and eroticism destroy a benighted population. Still others have seen him as an existentialist manqué, or as a keen observer of the violent streak in American life. Few American writers have inspired so much, and such fruitless, effort at critical description and classification, an effort that in itself suggests how seriously Caldwell was once perceived.

Most frequently he has been recognized, like Faulkner, as a writer whose chronicles of southern gothic horrors were profoundly metaphorical. Indeed, Faulkner himself praised Caldwell lavishly on a number of occasions, once calling him "America's greatest writer." Thus, although he has slipped from the high position he once held, enduring sales of his books and his former prominence assure a place in American literature, however minor and ambiguous it may be. In this respect, he surpasses such earlier popular writers as Booth Tarkington or Gertrude Atherton, who have faded permanently from view, but he can be more closely compared to Farrell or Cabell, both of whom made significant contributions to American fiction, though the bulk of their work is no longer held in particularly high repute.

To admit readily, as I do, that Caldwell's critical decline seems largely justified is not to admit that he is unworthy of study. For though Caldwell's best work is minor, it is by no means trivial; thus it is difficult to understand why he has not aroused more interest.

In the last dozen years, only two important long essays in English on Caldwell have appeared: James Korges's monograph published in the American Writers series of the University of Minnesota and Malcolm Cowley's perceptive and nostalgic chapter, "Georgia Boy," in *And I Worked at the Writer's Trade*—both titles that would certainly delight Caldwell. *Erskine Caldwell* will, I hope, at least partly correct a long-standing injustice.

Although Korges's work offers genuine insight into Caldwell and I have profited greatly from reading it, I feel nevertheless that too often he falls victim to puffery and critical overkill, invoking abtruse concepts to discuss such admittedly inferior books as *All Night Long* (1942).

If one is convinced that *All Night Long* is bad, "one of the worst novels I have ever read," as one reviewer wrote in desperation, then one must either say so bluntly or ignore the book for a better one. Such, at any rate, has been my conviction in the preparation of *Erskine Caldwell*. Caldwell ought not to receive applause where he has not earned it. Therefore I shall have little to say about most of those works that persist, in paperback, in the wire racks of drugstores and shopping centers, adorned by suggestive front covers invariably alluding to *God's Little Acre* or *Tobacco Road* and boasting blurbs either written years ago or excerpted from the minor newspapers that still review his books.

Instead of approaching Caldwell from the standard historical perspective as a writer whose lengthy career has been a long, unfulfilled promise, I prefer at this late date in his life to treat him as the author of several novels of real value and of a number of durable and accomplished short stories. I think that this productive writer—and on occasion a figure of genuine ability—should be more adequately understood two generations after his greatest triumphs. Further, I believe that his writing requires a study that offers a comprehensive analysis and evaluation of his best work, rather than a recondite treatment of some limited aspect of it. There is no lurking suspicion in my mind that Caldwell has somehow been denied his rightful place in American letters as the result of critical ignorance, or that under the proper conditions a Caldwell revival is possible. Rather, I propose only that Caldwell should be recognized as an important minor figure in the broad tradition of American naturalism. A product of the Southern Renaissance, among the most notable movements in modern American letters, he captured the imagination of scholar and casual reader alike with the uniqueness of his characters and motifs. He succeeded in combining the objective narrative stance of naturalism with the intimate depiction of emotion and irrationality that characterizes the modern antihero. In some respects he is among the earliest

American practitioners of twentieth-century black humor. Nothing human is alien to him. What Ronald Martin has said about the once popular Joseph Hergesheimer applies even more aptly to Erskine Caldwell: "Where his art has failings the particular failings are instructive. They illuminate some of the factors which define a writer as a minor writer. They also help to reveal the relationship between commercial and serious fiction and to show some of the effects of popular success on a dedicated author."

Biographically I have had to make do as best I could. If and when Caldwell's biography is ever published—one has existed without a publisher for more than a half dozen years—some errors and lacunae will surely manifest themselves. Caldwell is a private person who has resisted for many years interrogations both about his private life and his finances. In the period of his greatest popularity, he sometimes told gullible reporters and interviewers whoppers, often waggishly but sometimes from a less good-natured spirit. In this respect, he differs little from Hemingway, Faulkner, and his acquaintance Nathanael West, all of whom did the same and "made trouble for their biographers," as Malcolm Cowley has dryly noted who was himself a victim on several occasions.

This book, then, will be chiefly concerned with Caldwell's best fiction, mainly his novels—though some short stories will be mentioned from time to time. Of his other work, largely reportage and travel literature, little will be said. In writing *Erskine Caldwell,* my guiding purpose has been to remember that while his lesser efforts may often illuminate his triumphs, they must never detract from his accomplishments nor be allowed to stand as a measure of his worth. Of course, it will not be possible to ignore the extraordinary difference in quality between books written within a short period of time, or to ask oneself how the author of a good piece of writing could conceivably be capable of such a bad one, even years later; and from time to time I shall hazard opinions on this subject, especially because my view varies from the common judgment that Caldwell simply sold out. Although I have little to say about his inferior fiction, I am aware that the very existence of bad writing demands continual evaluation of the good. I propose here to offer a long overdue evaluation and analysis of a living author whose contribution to our literature still remains to be determined.

Finally, I am grateful to many for their aid in the writing of this book. I should especially like to thank Sheldon Grebstein, my *Dok-*

torvater, for his endless encouragement and a myriad of practical suggestions. Thanks are due also to Roger B. White for the use of his sister's wonderful photograph of Caldwell, to Gunter Narr Verlag for granting permission to incorporate into chapter 3 much of an article I published in 1979 in *Arbeiten aus Anglistik und Amerikanistik,* and to New American Library for allowing me to quote several paragraphs.

James E. Devlin

State University of New York
College at Oneonta

Chronology

1902   Caldwell born 17 December in Newnan, Coweta County, Georgia, to Ira Sylvester Caldwell, a minister of the Associate Reformed Presbyterian Church, and Caroline Preston Bell Caldwell, their only child.

1920   Graduates from Wrens Institute in Georgia. Begins freshman classes in September at Erskine College, Due West, South Carolina.

1921–1923   Leaves Erskine College in his sophomore year. String reporter for various newspapers.

1923–1927   Registers at University of Virginia; attends irregularly.

1925   Marries Helen Lannigan, three children (divorced 1938). Reporter on *Atlanta Journal*.

1926   Leaves Georgia for Maine.

1929   Breaks into print in the little magazines with "Joe Craddock's Old Woman" in *Blues* and "July" (a version of "Midsummer Passion") in *transition*. Alfred Kreymborg publishes "Midsummer Passion" in *The New American Caravan*. *The Bastard*, his first novel, appears.

1930   "The Bogus Ones," unpublished novella about a struggling writer in northern New England (this date is uncertain). Maxwell Perkins accepts "The Mating of Marjorie" and "A Very Late Spring" for publication in *Scribner's Magazine*. Second novel, *Poor Fool*, is published.

1931   Scribner's publishes *American Earth*, a short story collection. Works on *Tobacco Road* in New York for several weeks in the Sutton Hotel.

1932   *Tobacco Road* published by Scribner's Sons. Leaves Scribner's for Viking in dispute over next novel, *A Lamp for Nightfall*, published twenty years later.

1933   *Tobacco Road*, dramatized by Jack Kirkland, opens to mixed reviews but runs for more than seven years and 3,182 performances. Viking publishes *We Are the Living,* second story collection. *God's Little Acre* published by Viking. *Yale Review* award for story "County Full of Swedes." New York Society for the Suppression of Vice brings charges against *God's Little Acre.*

1933–1934 MGM scriptwriter.

1935 *Journeyman.*

1936 Tours South with Margaret Bourke-White, photographer.

1937 *You Have Seen Their Faces,* text by Caldwell with photographs by Bourke-White.

1938 *Journeyman* fails on the stage.

1938–1941 Foreign correspondent in numerous countries. Caldwell and Bourke-White in Soviet Union when Germans invade Russia.

1939 Marries Bourke-White (divorced 1942).

1940 Darryl Zanuck, head of production at Twentieth Century–Fox, purchases rights for *Tobacco Road* for $200,000. John Ford directs.

1941 Movie, *Tobacco Road* appears.

1941–1955 Editor, *American Folkways* series.

1942 *All Night Long,* propagandistic war novel, published and rights purchased by MGM. Marries June Johnson (divorced 1956).

1942–1943 Scriptwriter for Warner Brothers, Twentieth Century–Fox.

1943 *Georgia Boy* published by Duell, Sloan and Pearce; stage version fails. *Tragic Ground* banned in Boston. Hollywood salutes a wartime ally with *Mission to Moscow;* Caldwell's name does not appear on credits for "political reasons."

1944 Makes war bond rally tour.

1946 *God's Little Acre* reaches sales of 4.5 million.

1957 Marries Virginia Moffet Fletcher.

1958   Movie, *God's Little Acre* appears.

1961   Movie, *Claudelle Inglish* appears.

1965   *In Search of Bisco.*

1975   Operated on a second time for lung cancer.

1976   *Afternoons in Mid-America.*

Chapter One
Caldwell's Life, Career, and Aesthetic: An Overview

Life

Erskine Preston Caldwell was born in 1902 in Newnan, Georgia, a small town about forty miles from Atlanta.[1] In later years, like so many other writers, he did little to discourage the dissemination of romantic but wildly inaccurate accounts of his youth and young manhood. In fact, both were fairly prosaic. His father, a minister of the small Associate Reformed Presbyterian Church, was a self-reliant farm boy who studied his Greek and Latin four years at Erskine College, Due West, South Carolina, before enlisting for service in Cuba. Upon his discharge from the Hornets' Nest Riflemen, a North Carolina company, he returned to Due West and the theological seminary at Erskine College. The year after his ordination, he married a young woman he had met there, who came from a good Virginia family and was an instructor at the Women's College. He took his bride back to the parish house of White Oak Associate Reformed Presbyterian Church in Newnan, where he was already serving as minister and where his son was born.

The young Caldwell moved with his parents to a succession of small southern towns, where his father, an unusually diplomatic and conciliatory figure, was sent by the church to mend pastoral fences or soothe the troubled waters of contentious congregations. These frequent removals kept his formal education sketchy, but that deficiency was largely remedied by instruction from his mother, who had taught Latin and French, and by his father, who often taught high school to supplement his meager clerical income. As secretary of the Home Missions Board, the Reverend Ira Sylvester Caldwell zigzagged through the Carolinas, Tennessee, Virginia, and Florida from one rural church to another, where dour-faced farmers of Scotch descent paid their minister in meat, flour, and sugar as often as in money, before settling permanently in 1919, in Wrens, Georgia, a town of twelve hundred people thirty-five miles south of Augusta. There the senior Caldwell accepted the pastorate of the Associate Reformed Presbyterian Church, a position he held more than three decades until his death in 1944. In his last years, his son's widespread notoriety seems to have been a matter of some personal satisfaction to him, and he thoroughly enjoyed disappointing those reporters and visitors who expected to find in Erskine Caldwell's father an illiterate, wild-eyed country preacher.

Wrens was the closest thing to a hometown that Caldwell ever had. It was here as a teenager that he found a job with the *Jefferson Reporter,* a paper whose casual editor-owner gave him full responsibility for writing, setting up, and distributing the six-page, six-hundred-copy weekly before going off on vacation. When Caldwell was finally able to broach the subject of seven weeks' back wages to the returned owner, he was told that the opportunity to learn "newspapering" should be payment enough and warned that so much concern for money and so little for loyalty boded only ill. He promptly quit. But this experience infected him with a genuine *furor scribendi.* Longing to see his work in print again, he next managed with some difficulty to become a baseball string correspondent for some Augusta, Macon, and even Atlanta dailies. Only small portions of what he wrote, however, ever reached the newspapers; nonetheless he continued to write accounts of baseball games and news stories from provincial Wrens for several years. His tenuous connections with newspapers would continue until 1926, when, after almost a year, he left the *Atlanta Journal* to learn the creative writer's craft.

While still living in Wrens, the young Caldwell became familiar with the back country west of the Savannah River, where many years earlier cured tobacco was rolled in hogsheads along "tobacco roads" down to the river. As a chauffeur for a doctor and then a tax assessor, and later as a companion to his father on pastoral visits, the young Caldwell met the tenant farmers living on the dusty dirt roads miles from the crossroad stores. Their houses, he saw, were often one- or two-room shacks with some beds or pallets, an iron stove, and a few chairs. Desolate and decaying, they stood behind the weed-bordered road, surrounded by fields now planted in cotton but where, years earlier before the soil gave out, rich crops of tobacco had grown. He felt a profound sorrow for these hopeless people and approved the small charities his father and the doctor were able to offer them; at the same time he was struck by the difference between them and himself. Their world was not his. He asked his father what would become of them and their numerous children, but Ira Caldwell could not supply an answer.[2]

Aware that though he could feel sympathy for their plight, he could never really apprehend life as they did, he would seek later to make his poor whites and blacks understandable to readers without attempting to win their empathy, a goal that Bertolt Brecht called the *Verfremdungseffekt,* or alienation effect. Like Caldwell, he too sought to expose ignorance, impoverishment, and prejudice without engaging his audience's deepest emotions so that it might concentrate more objectively on the problems he presented.[3]

But living in Wrens was largely a happy period for Caldwell. Here he finished two successive years of high school, the kind of sustained educational experience that had been rare in the past and would remain so in the future. Though he lacked credits enough to graduate, it was nonetheless decided he could enroll at Erskine College, his father's alma mater, a small school affiliated with the Associate Reformed Presbyterian Church and named after the Scottish dissenter Ebenezer Erskine. The redoubtable eighteenth-century preacher's namesake arrived to begin freshman classes at Erskine College in September 1920, where he appears to have enjoyed the extracurricular aspects of collegiate life more than the somewhat restraining discipline of the institution. He was interested in football, girls, and adhering to the modified fagging system the college boasted. But he also began hopping freights on weekends to explore the surrounding country, taking care he did not travel so far that he was unable to return by Sunday night or early Monday morning. This urge to move about his own country and to exotic corners of Eastern Europe and other distant spots remained a lifelong passion. At least ten of Caldwell's books would eventually be devoted to travel, and he would always take great pride in his general editorship of the *American Folkways* series, a collection of studies of regional America by a variety of American writers.

By Christmas vacation of his sophomore year, Caldwell was ready to set out on his own. He headed toward New Orleans like young Sam Clemens, looking not for a ship to take him to the Amazon but for a Gulf of Mexico freighter. However, he had as little success in his venture as Clemens did and was subsequently arrested in Bogalusa, Louisiana, after falling behind a week in his room rent. In the

1930s, this incident, greatly exaggerated, would be cited as evidence of his colorful early life. But it must have left a lasting impression on Caldwell since he mentioned it often. For the first time in his life, he found himself in the position of the wretched souls he would write about. Twice a day, a resigned middle-aged black trusty came to the teenager's cell with greens and fatback. Each time Caldwell asked him if he knew why he was being kept and how long he would be held. But to the black, injustice was a way of life. Nothing surprised him, and he saw no reason to become involved in an affair that might compromise him. "You better ask the white folks, boss," he said evasively, though he admitted, "I sure know how you feel . . . because I feel like I've been locked up in here all my life my own self."[4]

Some days later, Caldwell was able to write a letter to his father and push it out the barred window to a small black boy, who bought a stamp and mailed it in return for the change left over from a nickel thrown to him. In another day, a YMCA secretary, contacted by his father, secured Caldwell's release. After a shower, change of clothes, and a hot meal, Caldwell sat in a train about to head home, studying a large billboard warning "wobblies" and other labor agitators of the treatment they might expect in Bogalusa.

For a brief interval, Caldwell happily resumed string reporting local news events from Wrens for city papers. But soon he felt an appetite for college again. This time he wanted no part of Erskine College; he sought instead a large university. But because of his parents' limited means and his mediocre record, his ambition seemed unattainable until he discovered an obscure scholarship offered by the United Daughters of the Confederacy to a resident of the state of Georgia descended from a Confederate soldier.

At the University of Virginia, Caldwell found himself most interested in sociology and English. He began writing class assignments for these courses as sketches and stories, though neither form was especially appropriate. He also wrote poems and jokes for the *Virginia Reel* and submitted the rejects to national humor magazines for a dollar each. At Virginia he met Charles Wertenbaker, a student already writing a novel, and James Aswell, both of whom acquired small reputations later. He also met a book shop owner, Gordon Lewis, who told him he would help publish Caldwell's work if it looked meritorious and salable.

Dizzied by the heady atmosphere of the Southern Renaissance now permeating the University of Virginia, Caldwell grew obsessed with writing. He changed courses, seeking inspiration, and even dropped out of the university temporarily.

I knew how I wanted to write and what I wanted to write about. I wanted to write about the people I knew as they really lived, moved, and talked. During the four years that I was an in-and-out student at Virginia, only two years of which were actually spent in residence, I worked a milk delivery route for a while in Washington, D.C., spent several months working behind the counter in an orange drink stand in Philadelphia, and was for four months a stock clerk in charge of crockery and glassware in the basement of a variety store in Wilkes-Barre, Pennsylvania.[5]

In 1925, the year the *Virginia Quarterly Review* first appeared, Caldwell left Charlottesville and took a job with the *Atlanta Journal,* a paper he had once served as a baseball string correspondent.[6] Newspaper life taught him what it had taught Dreiser, Hemingway, and O'Hara. He learned how to write quickly, pointedly, and forcefully, while achieving a certain confidence in himself and absorbing the cynical distrust that reporters felt for literary men. But he became more convinced, too, that he was destined to be one of them, and he began writing stories on the side. Further, he reviewed books for other papers, a practice he would continue for a long time after leaving the *Journal* the next year.

Despite the irresolute course of his life to this point, Caldwell had grown continually more serious about his writing, and inspired by an almost Calvinistic sense of calling, he began to set goals for himself as a writer. He had started also to formulate the critical theory that would serve him for the rest of his life. He knew that he wanted to be a creative writer and resolved to work single-mindedly at that ambition for a period of ten years. He had come to believe that a successful writer must be a "good" writer, and, as in the newspaper world, that sales were an important indication of success. In reviewing books by the boxful, he concluded there was too little time in life both to read books and to write them, and that he would rather write them. He resolved to abandon reviewing at the first chance. In addition to teaching him the value of short words and a blunt style, newspaper experience aroused his hostility toward anything as theoretical as the formal study of literature. He was already a critic himself, and he did not think much of the breed—"impotent lovers" he later called them.[7]

Now twenty-four and newly married, Caldwell quit the city room of the *Journal* and left the South. His choice of exile, rural Maine, was deliberate. Europe had no charms for a novice writer who had been too young for the war and who was little interested in history, art, music, or languages. Though he had not yet quite decided what he would write about, Maine seemed to offer the sanctuary he needed, a new aspect of the unhurried rural America he liked best. There would be plenty of time for writing in Maine. Here, with his wife and family, Caldwell carried out a long apprenticeship on his way to "overnight success."

Career

Caldwell's Maine years belong more properly to his "career" than his "life," since he saw his first story published and earned his first income, in his phrase, as a "writer of fiction," during his Maine residence. Although he continued until 1928 to review books for southern papers and even ran a bookstore in Portland staffed by a recent Smith graduate and stocked with review copies, Caldwell concentrated on writing short fiction. Since his academic training was weak, he depended upon his instinct, which in most cases was good. He sought for each story an "intensity of feeling," a quality not very different from Poe's "intensity of effect," and to instill confidence, he pretended that "no one else would ever read" his stories but himself. He was cautiously attracted to the innocent narrator, whose breathless naiveté, a vestige of Twain's and Sherwood Anderson's narrative technique, became a standard component of the short story in the twenties and thirties but which has proved a liability to writers with less talent than a Eudora Welty or J. D. Salinger.[8]

He sought eclectically the ingredients that suited him in the short story as it evolved from Chekhov through Anderson and Hemingway. His dependence upon the epiphany suggests the influence of Joyce, though both the epiphany and the anecdote, a legacy of various sources, were later to handicap him in his practices as a novelist. For the bawdy element of so many short stories, he is undoubtedly indebted to the *Droll Stories* of Balzac, whom he often mentioned along with de Maupassant when questioned about writers he admired. Certainly he knew and imitated the ribald fabliau; this favorite comic situation of an onlooker witnessing the sexual activities of others may have come to him from *Troilus and Criseyde* where "Chaucer, a master of the lusty yarn of fabliau, used his masterpiece of characterization, Pandarus, in the exact situation employed by the Georgia author."⁹

Early Stories

Caldwell's earliest published stories are extraordinarily uneven. He experimented with first and third person narrations. He alternated between southern and Maine settings. He attempted tough, naturalistic city settings, producing mawkish things like "Dorothy" (1931), and repeatedly tried his hands at themes of sexual awakening in adolescence. Most of these latter attempts, like "Strawberry Season" (1930), are saved from sentimentality by a realistic depiction of adolescent confusion and psychic turbulence. Some early stories deal with the plight of blacks and introduce Caldwell's version of the "grotesque" character. Many of the best, like "Midsummer Passion," his first accepted story, are anecdotal accounts of irrational behavior. They tend to be stories in the Ring Lardner vein that one might imagine being told in a barbershop of a small town, involving a well-known local character at a critical point in his life, almost as in a Browning monologue, or at his most irrational or stubbornest. The epiphany of stories like these must take place in the reader's mind rather than in the character himself. We deduce from them only that man is far from a rational being, let alone civilized or "Christian." The stories are droll but seldom truly funny. They also develop a casual attitude toward violence and frequently maintain an almost irritatingly neutral perspective. Caldwell, in fact, became so adept at this narrative guise that many readers and critics considered him, if not slightly stupid, then nearly indifferent to human suffering. What they failed to realize is that this pretense of indifference was a fundamental aspect of Caldwell's craft.

It was during these Maine years, in 1929, that Caldwell received a letter from Alfred Kreymborg accepting for publication "Midsummer Passion" in *The New American Caravan,* an annual of American literature and criticism. Unknown to Caldwell, who had been mailing out this story and others to little magazines, one of the most prestigious, *transition,* had also printed the story in Paris under a different title. Kreymborg's acceptance encouraged Caldwell enormously, and he began submitting his stories in large numbers to *Blues, Hound and Horn, Nativity,* and *Pagany,* gradually placing a few. These successes put him into the company of the country's most accomplished writers. Soon Maxwell Perkins of Scribner's expressed interest in his work, and Caldwell immediately submitted a sheaf of stories he had written since leaving Georgia.

About this time, Caldwell had published two novelettes through small presses, *The Bastard* (1929) and *Poor Fool* (1930). In later years, he seldom mentioned either book, though he never specifically disowned them. It is frankly difficult to find a single redeeming feature in them. Both not only are inferior works but even hint at a disturbed state of mind in their author. The hero of each book is "tough," but shows less debt to the alienated, though highly responsible protagonists of Hemingway, than to the kind of hero that writers like Dashiell Hammett and the *Black Mask* magazine school were inventing. *Poor Fool* is essentially a big-city crime story, sensational in its lurid scenes of necrophilia, obviously inspired by the pulps. Both books also contain the mother figure who looms so large in Caldwell's later fiction. This older woman, who is often depicted as obese, appears in both malevolent and kindly form, always exhibiting domineering traits and sometimes an offensive sexuality. Her reappearance in novels like *The Sure Hand of God* (1947), *Jenny by Nature* (1961), and *Miss Mama Aimee* (1967) may be sadly considered a *regressus ad uterum*.

During the same years that Caldwell wrote *The Bastard* and *Poor Fool*, he wrote a very different short novel which he was unable to have published then or later, despite making several attempts.[10] According to Guy Owen, "The Bogus Ones" is a semiautobiographical novel "of a struggling young writer" living in Maine. While "the plight of the artists in a materialistic society" is its chief theme, an ancillary one concerns the "distrust of sex in art and fiction" displayed by "life-denying" New Englanders. Caldwell, who himself encountered censorship problems with *The Bastard* in Maine, includes in "The Bogus Ones" a scene in which the writer-protagonist Fritz Mann is subjected to a bookstore owner's tirade against a novel of D. H. Lawrence. Owen finds "The Bogus Ones" flat, unconvincing, and humorless, but also revealing about a period in Caldwell's life of which he has been quite reticent, and interesting in its foreshadowing of the frank treatment of sexual themes in his later novels.

What Caldwell sought next was "to break down the editorial resistance of *Scribner's Magazine*." It took him three months to accomplish that; but in March of 1930 Maxwell Perkins sent word that he had decided to publish a story. Caldwell rushed off to New York, bringing three more he had just written, of which Perkins eventually agreed to accept two.[11] Caldwell remembered vividly his first experience with Perkins, and years later liked to tell how he sold "The Mating of Marjorie" and "A Very Late Spring," two New England stories with a distinct Sherwood Anderson flavor. He had been called by Perkins on the telephone a day after leaving them at the Scribner's office without daring to ask for Perkins himself. After some congenial small talk, Perkins offered Caldwell "two-fifty" for both stories. Caldwell was dumbfounded. Perkins increased the offer to "three-fifty." Caldwell agreed, adding that "three dollars and a half" still seemed low to him. The diplomatic Perkins, a wily Vermont Yankee who knew the value of a dollar himself, explained that he meant "three hundred fifty dollars."

In June of 1930, the two stories appeared in *Scribner's Magazine,* but Caldwell found that this did not necessarily mean that *Scribner's* was permanently open to him. Luckily, he had concluded in the meantime that the schooling of the literary and experimental magazines was a valuable experience, and they, at any rate, continued to accept his stories. In July of that year, determined to make a fresh start, he burned three suitcases full of manuscripts, essays, jokes, critical writings, poems, and stories dating back to 1923.[12] Not long after this dramatic gesture Scribner's suggested publishing a collection of his stories to be called *American Earth* (1931). But at the same time Perkins warned him that novels sold better than story collections.

The Busy Years

Accordingly, Caldwell left Maine on an extended cross-country trip that eventually brought him to Georgia, where he roamed the countryside observing the effects of the Depression on the rural populace. Then he returned to New York to write *Tobacco Road,* an impression of the Georgia backcountry recollected in tranquility. Though Scribner's accepted *Tobacco Road* immediately, they were not favorably impressed by his next effort, a work he usually calls his "Maine novel" (published twenty years later as *A Lamp for Nightfall*). Their refusal to take it brought him to Viking, with whom he published *God's Little Acre* in 1933. With the growing notoriety of Jack Kirkland's dramatization of *Tobacco Road* early in 1934, Caldwell's name became increasingly well known.

And yet his writing had begun to encounter difficulty though neither he nor the public was aware of it yet. Sales of *Tobacco Road* and
God's Little Acre continued to burgeon, and Hollywood, which had
had him on the payroll the previous year for an ill-fated bayou saga
set in Louisiana, was whispering seductively again. But his next novels and many of his short stories would be less warmly received.
Nonetheless, in the busy year of 1934, there seemed little to worry
about. True, he had not written "a book for publication" that year,
a serious failing in his eyes, but he had a successful and profitable
play running on Broadway, which was producing royalties of about
one hundred dollars a week in the shakiest of economic times. If his
marriage was crumbling in Maine, his pen seemed as prolific as ever
and he succeeded in writing a half dozen new stories from as many
hotel rooms in as many cities, among them "Kneel to the Rising
Sun" in which he felt a justifiable faith. Further he had in mind a
new novel about an itinerant unordained preacher.

He finished *Journeyman* about the middle of May and worked that
summer in California on a never-to-be-produced film, driving back
East in a brand new car at the end of the Hollywood assignment until
he reached Georgia where he gathered material for his tract *Tenant
Farmer*. In the fall he lectured to English classes at Columbia and
New York University, chose stories for his new collection *Kneel to the
Rising Sun,* and traveled to Chicago where it was optimistically
thought his presence might somehow influence Mayor Edward J.
Kelly or the courts to revoke the ban there on a touring company's
production of *Tobacco Road.*

When Viking was unwilling to publish his nonfiction observation
of life in the United States entitled *Some American People,* his agent
Max Lieber took it to another publisher. Caldwell now grew eager to
try his hand again at more journalism, a love he had never lost, and
Lieber, mindful of his client's passion, his thousands of miles of recent travel, and the "progressive" tone of both *Tenant Farmer* and
Some American People, suggested a new book, a "study of people in the
cotton states living under current economic stress."[13]

In the meantime, Lieber arranged for Caldwell to journey South
again in the winter of 1935 to prepare two series of articles on tenant
farms for the *New York Post,* the last of which was published in the
spring of that year. In 1935, too, *Journeyman* came out to generally
unenthusiastic reviews, but the royalties from the stage version of

Tobacco Road swelled to almost ten times the previous year's, about a thousand dollars a week.

In 1936, Caldwell saw through a private printing of his impressionistic prose poem *The Sacrilege of Alan Kent,* while Lieber, whose interest in leftish causes evoked charges against him years later from Whitaker Chambers, brought about a meeting between Caldwell and the "bright, gallant, ambitious, and hard-working"[14] Margaret Bourke-White, a talented young photographer just coming into prominence for a volume of photographs on the New Russia. The two set off for a tour of the South, a collaborative effort that would result in the acclaimed photo-essay published the next year, *You Have Seen Their Faces.*

From this point on, Caldwell was constantly in the company of Margaret Bourke-White. Malcolm Cowley lyrically describes the pair at a mid-Manhattan hotel meeting in behalf of a no longer recalled left-wing cause: "Those two, absorbed in each other, gave focus and form to the slovenly meeting, while we others had become the wilderness in which they gleamed."[15] Caldwell, however, had begun to do almost as much journalism as creative writing. He took on a lecture assignment and then bowed out of it. He promised *Midweek Pictorial* a story a week but found the pace too demanding after a dozen efforts. For Viking he oversaw the compilation of stories for *Southways,* his fourth short story collection. At the same time he checked over and made changes in a script for the dramatization of *Journeyman,* sinking into the play almost ten thousand dollars before the production closed in its third week.

With Margaret Bourke-White, he visited central Europe in the early summer of 1938 on the eve of World War II to collect material for another photo-essay, *North of the Danube,* and would collaborate twice again with her in the near future: *Say, Is This the USA* (1941) and *Russia at War* (1942). The war itself, however, gave sudden impetus to his flagging literary career. Not only did American GIs devour enormous quantities of *Tobacco Road* and *God's Little Acre*[16] but through their agency Caldwell's work was eventually introduced into Germany and Japan. Meanwhile, Caldwell involved himself in a number of war efforts in addition to preparing more short story collections. From Russia and England he reported and broadcast on the war, often on trips with Margaret Bourke-White whom he married in 1939, and still found time to dash off a novel about heroic Russian partisans struggling against brutal Nazi invaders. He was now general editor of the *American Folkways* series, appearing on radio, writing periodically for *Life* magazine, working for the movies, and even selling war bonds with other celebrities.

In Retrospect

But the end of the war also marked the end of Caldwell's critical acclaim. His popular decline came much more slowly. He continued to publish prolifically and attract a goodly share of publicity. But this sort of fame could not conceal the fact that the still youthful Caldwell was slipping. The total failure of the dramatization of *Georgia Boy* in 1945 served as a tocsin to his diminishing promise. Certainly the concluding five novels of his "cyclorama" of the South, written after the war, represented a distinct falling off in power and were largely ignored by critics who had once regarded him as rivaling Faulkner.

No longer a favorite of the little magazines where he had appeared beside such avant-garde figures as Gertrude Stein, Wallace Stevens, William Carlos Williams, and Langston Hughes; and dropped from the elite company of Hemingway, Fitzgerald, and Faulkner, which he had briefly shared in the pages of *Scribner's,* Caldwell was now becoming a "pop" writer who appeared in department and drugstores to sign books and promote the new paper editions—to an undiscriminating audience. Though he continued to write novels as well as perceptive studies of race relations and southern religion, and works of autobiography and criticism, his efforts did not reawaken critical interest. But unlike a Hamlin Garland whose bleak early vision of the world about him sweetened with material success, Caldwell never abandoned his commitment to the downtrodden for a more cheerful view of life; he remained true to his deeper vision. When his writing declined in quality and his interest in politics flagged, he maintained his moral indignation and indeed fanned it by concentrating frequently on the plight of the southern black. Like Hemingway he came to bristle at unfriendly criticism. But since he was never the great public figure that Hemingway had been, he found it easier to turn into himself, to retreat into strong self-reliance and trust in his instinct. His public statements continued to belittle the formal study of literature as airily impractical, and stressed craftsmanship, self-discipline, and experience at the expense of academic strictures untested in the marketplace of public approval. He also bluntly reiterated his belief that a writer does best to ignore the fickle reviewers who offer him adulation one day and rebuffs the next.

The discovery that the South and particularly rural Georgia were to be the shaping factors of his creative imagination came slowly to Caldwell. Although he thought, during his student days at the University of Virginia, that he knew what he wanted to write about, namely, "the people I knew as they really lived, moved, and talked,"[17] his words display an empty bravado on at least two counts. First, although he showed a predictable partiality to literary realism, he does not disclose the depth of his attraction to other modes, notably expressionism and impressionism, nor does he indicate the distrust he felt for conventional or "photographic realism." Even at this time he was willing to admit he "was not writing about real people . . . but about the acts and desires of imaginary ones who . . . were so convincingly depicted that they should seem more like actual persons than living ones would be."[18] This distinction shows that Caldwell understood some of the limitations of photographic realism, though it does not much clarify the symbolic movement of his writing. Second, he says nothing specific about the subjects of his prose. Who are "the people" he "knew" and in what sense did Caldwell "know" them? To what extent did Caldwell know the backcountry Georgia folk that he had always observed at a distance or visited in the company of authoritative outsiders? No one would argue, however, that he knew them better than the boxers, gangsters, and French Canadians he sometimes chose to write about.

At the beginning of his career, then, Caldwell was actually very uncertain about both the method and subject of his writing. While he leaned toward a form of realism, he understood clearly that mere reportage of events and characters did not in itself embody the truth he wanted to express; he realized that imagination played a role in storytelling that he would somehow have to exploit. His solution was ultimately the "symbolic naturalism" of *Tobacco Road* and, to a lesser extent, *God's Little Acre,* but for a time he flirted with expressionism, and traces of it remain in many of his novels and stories. *The Sacrilege of Alan Kent,* on the other hand, published in 1936 but written in three parts in 1929, 1930, and 1931, is almost wholly impressionistic.

Influenced by the themes and character types of Sherwood Anderson, by the dialogue and style of Hemingway, and by the storytelling tradition of the Old South as personified for him in his grandfather, Caldwell never settled permanently into a fixed pattern. *The Bastard* and *Poor Fool* utilize eerie and dangerous city settings, which show not so much the influence of Dreiser as they do the postwar expressionists and the pulp magazines. Deliberately, but never wholly consistently, he came to write about lower levels of rural society. The failure to interest either Scribner's or Viking in his "Maine novel," despite the success of *Tobacco Road* and *God's Little Acre,* doubtless contributed to Caldwell's belief that he would do best to write about the South. Much later he would often refer to his "cyclorama of southern life," signifying the ten or eleven novels with southern themes beginning with *Tobacco Road* and ending with *Episode in Palmetto* (1950), implying that they constituted a chronicle of life in the modern South. Although this appellation—and its implied claim— may well have been an afterthought, it indicates that two decades after his most enthusiastic recognition and after prolonged absence from the South, Caldwell still thought of himself as chiefly a southern writer. On the other hand, readers of Caldwell will find that the term is pretentious in many respects. Certainly this "cyclorama" cannot be compared to Faulkner's (much less Zola's) series, which is intricately linked and encompasses a broad span of years with historical and psychological sweep. Nor does it resemble the loosely organized *Human Comedy* of Balzac or the extended treatments of a single protagonist like those of James T. Farrell. Moreover, when he strays from what might be called "Caldwell country," as he necessarily does in half of these novels, the result is often unhappy.

Critical Theory

But if he was in practice sometimes unsure about his own purpose, he seldom betrayed the same uncertainty in discussing the theory of writing or criticism. His notion of the function of criticism is highly intolerant. He depicted critics in such terms as "bloated middlemen" or "impotent lovers." At their meddling worst, they are personified by the contemptible character he created in 1940 for *Jackpot,* the imaginary Professor Horatio Perkins; at their best, they are something like Alexander Woollcott, the bête noire of New York in the twenties and thirties. Though Caldwell, like others, was impressed by Woollcott's suavity and hit it off well with him personally, Woollcott typified for him the tyrannical critic whose biting wit and ponderous presence could overawe struggling author and naive reader alike. The fictional Perkins, on the other hand, is. a parasite pure and simple.

Living off the work of better men, "tearing flesh from the bone" with a bloodless smile, he seeks "the secret of writing fiction," as ineffable a formula as ever existed. Between the living, fire-breathing Woollcott and the fantastic devourer of stolen meat, Perkins, Caldwell conceived a hateful army of others he held in varying degrees of contempt.

Despite this contempt, and perhaps because he spent so many years as reviewer himself, Caldwell devoted almost as much energy to issuing critical dicta as he did to attacking critics. His own criticism is not always consistent, though it is certainly eclectic. On occasion he paraphrases a number of the most revered classical critics, including Horace and Aristotle, while his attitude toward the practical business of writing and publishing is downright Johnsonian. Nonetheless, his most characteristic attitudes are romantic rather than classical. He is extremely ambiguous on a number of key critical issues, almost as if he accepts simultaneously both their thesis and antithesis.

For example, he believes with good reason that authorship is hard work, that one learns by doing, and that inspiration or innate talent—"natural ability," in his words—though essential, is only the beginning of the writing process. In the Horatian mode he exclaims: "It is doubtful if anyone who has published a short story or novel attained that distinction without first serving an apprenticeship lengthy or brief, but certainly of some duration."[19] Yet at the same time he has freely admitted to having no idea how stories would end before reaching their conclusions, and he constantly stresses the need for unrestricted imagination on the part of author and reader alike as an essential ingredient for the reading or writing of literature. He is further convinced that popularity is a sign of innate worth and that the writer must not only possess an inordinate amount of self-reliance but also trust his readers. "A writer's obligation," he says, "was to himself and to his readers. . . . readers were to be the ones to pass final judgment on my books."[20] His lack of concern with precedent is almost as great as his disinterest in style which, he feels, will take care of itself if the "content" is sufficiently good. By "content" he means plot (or at least situation) and characterization. His plots, however, as will later be demonstrated, remain sketchy or episodic throughout his career. Some of his characters, on the other hand, are enduring. In the creation of Jeeter Lester, Ty Ty Walden, Darling Jill, Candy-Man Beechum, and many others, he has made a permanent contribution to American literature.

His attitude toward his characters and the experiences they undergo is surprisingly sophisticated for a largely self-taught writer. Though in his autobiography, *Call It Experience* (1951), he could still avow his early belief in holding a mirror to life, we have already seen that Caldwell recognized the limitations of realism. Instead he turned to a "symbolic naturalism," a school identified by Caroline Gordon and Allen Tate, which John Bradbury in *Renaissance in the South* calls "the new tradition of the Southern novel and short story."[21] Though Bradbury would cavalierly dismiss Caldwell as a lurid sensationalist, Caldwell's work closely adheres to the tradition as Bradbury defines it: "a carefully detailed or 'naturalistic' surface, irony, symbolism, a strict and consistent handling of the point of view."[22] In drawing characters and situations expressive of real states of mind inside real experience, Caldwell lifted himself far above both carping critics and such still life realists as Edith Wharton or Willa Cather. In brief, he went beyond the classical theory of mimesis to a more inclusive and modern realization that the depths of human experience transcend "realism" as it had come down to American writers of the twentieth century. If grotesquerie served his purpose, he was exploiting only the same mode as Kafka and other characteristically "modern" writers. In some of his best work, there is a subtle but deliberate anti-realism, as there is in Zola or Steinbeck, which is almost purely expressionistic. But more often he shows a kinship to the non-Aristotelian perspective of a writer like the German Bertolt Brecht who is also loath—though less so than Caldwell—to reject realism completely.

Naturalism-Realism

In spite of his keen awareness of the limits of realism, Caldwell most often discussed his art—or "craft" as he usually calls it—in terms unambiguously belonging to the naturalistic-realistic tradition he knew best. He frequently stressed the necessity of returning to the South for firsthand experience with the backgrounds of his stories. In *Jackpot* he makes a statement reminiscent of Zola's concern with documentation: "A writer has to be a jack of all trades. He has to know how to harness a horse and snub a tractor; how to gig suckers and bait a taut-line; how to pick up a brick wall and shore up a cow shed. Furthermore, he has to know how to make crêpes Suzette and Sauerbraten; how to change a baby and shroud a corpse; how to float stock and sink a catamaran. Further still, he has to know how to recognize a Piquet frock and a Suzy hat; how to make love and how to practice celibacy; how to take time exposure and how to make a lap dissolve."[23]

Then, too, though he claimed as adamantly as Poe to despise didacticism in any form and protested strenuously that he served no cause, he wrote story after story pointing out the injustices suffered by the blacks and the poor. His championing of the tenant farmer in novels and nonfiction and of the Depression "stiff" in stories like "Slow Death" ("It is hardly necessary to point out that this story was written in the year 1932")[24] renders suspect his disclaimers of impartiality. His interest in families and heredity, the downtrodden, the influence of environment on character, the neurotic, and his cultivated objective narrative voice are other hallmarks of naturalism in the last hundred years.

Aesthetics

In addition to the readily apparent naturalistic base of Caldwell's work, with its overtones of biological determinism and the equally pessimistic absurdist note struck occasionally, there appears a strong romantic belief in the primacy of feeling. Caldwell's distrust of anything savoring of intellectualism is almost as complete as that of his characters. He often views sex, like D. H. Lawrence, as a liberating force bringing out the god in man, and of course, he believes in self-reliance as firmly as Emerson ever did. He insists that a special relationship exists between author and readers, wherein the former, self-reliant and filled with inspiration, provides an emotional stimulus that readers recognize and respond to. This force is beyond the appreciation of "Professor Perkins," who has cultivated his crammed head at the expense of his heart. The average person, whose imagination has not been perverted through excessive cerebralism, will infallibly recognize and respond to the emotional force of a good story. For this reason, the reader is to be relied upon almost as the voice of God. Thus, popularity becomes for Caldwell a standard by which excellence is judged.

His trust in the divine average sometimes leads him away from the pessimism one might expect from a determinist. In this respect, he resembles Steinbeck, whose fiction also recurrently asserts optimism. Both writers, like Faulkner, seem to believe that somehow humanity will prevail. Yet too much can be made of the rays of hope that shine dimly through *Tobacco Road* and *God's Little Acre*. Caldwell fully understood that "those enjoying the pleasant things in life are fewer than those enduring the unpleasant."[25] And even in his gentlest and drollest stories, he does not convey the impression that he is deliberately holding back his blackest vision. Instead, he seems only to be striking a realistic balance, as he once said, between the "depiction of the violent and ugly, of poverty and class conflict" and "spasms of laughter, the horseplay of humor, and the enjoyment of living."[26]

World View

Many of his best novels are nearly nihilistic, even if he has not always been unambiguous in the expression of his nihilism. *Tobacco Road,* for example, concludes with Dude Lester's wondering if "maybe I could grow me a bale to the acre, like Pa was always talking about doing." While this is hardly a strong affirmation of faith, it could conceivably be read as a positive statement from the hitherto irresponsible youth about man's will to struggle toward the fulfillment of old dreams. Such optimism will be short-lived if one recalls that Dude's father, Jeeter Lester, had said much the same thing for years. Moreover, the ambition is hopeless in the sandy east Georgia soil, as Caldwell explained in great detail some years later in his photo-essay with Margaret Bourke-White, *You Have Seen Their Faces* (1937). "A bale an acre" was a reasonable goal only for areas like the rich Mississippi Valley Delta or the Black Belt of Alabama.

God's Little Acre and *Journeyman* reflect the existentialist belief that reason is incapable of dealing with life. The first of these novels attempts to transform that defect into an asset by championing a new sexual ethic, taught by the life example of Will Thompson, a failed socialist, but charismatic figure. However, what is appropriate for this alienated superman fails to serve as a new morality for lesser mortals; and, indeed, *Journeyman* seems to negate Will's lesson by furnishing a lecherous protagonist almost as charismatic as the labor leader but without his social concern. In *God's Little Acre,* the mill strike Will leads fails, and the expression of a life force through sex leads only to death and disharmony in the Walden family. The last scene of that novel, almost a parody of Voltaire's *Candide,* shows Ty Ty Walden, patriarch of his little clan, turning to the earth to dig, not hopefully cultivating his garden, but irrationally indulging his obsession that in spite of all that has happened about him, gold may yet be discovered on his property.

Journeyman describes a retreat to a kind of hopeless stasis. Indeed, all the novels from *Tobacco Road* to *Tragic Ground* (1944), including even the bittersweet *Georgia Boy* (1943), conclude in a mood of deceptive calm, not the calm of passions spent that informs great tragedy, but rather a vacuous state that numbly follows the meaningless death of protagonists or other central characters.

The Southern Renaissance and Other Influences

For the student of literature, the term *Southern Renaissance* has become as much honorific as descriptive. To be identified with that elusive, though significant, movement bestows a certain instanteous recognition and prestige to an American writer. It is thus reasonable to inquire to what extent Caldwell might qualify for inclusion in a movement whose membership depends ultimately upon one's southern affiliation, if only by adoption or temporary residence.

The question is a difficult one since the Southern Renaissance is as much a state of mind as a school. It includes writers of great importance and of little, of vastly different styles, and at home in areas as different from each other as Maine is from Georgia. In Caldwell's case, a role in the Southern Renaissance might mean little more than witnessing the literary activity that flourished in the South after World War I, since Caldwell was a loner who eschewed schools and cliques and found his first success in isolation hundreds of miles from his home state. Of course, he was aware of the atmosphere at the University of Virginia, though he played no active part in what was going on about him. He was aware, too, of the awesome presence of Margaret Mitchell during his days on the *Atlanta Journal*, and her subsequent popular success with *Gone with the Wind* in 1936 would have seemed to him as evidence of her worth. By the same token, though he is separated from the style and content of Frances Newman by a yawning gulf, he was "deeply impressed" by *The Short Story's Mutations*, the collection Miss Newman edited in 1924, and emotionally moved by the very sight of the typescript for *The Hard-Boiled Virgin*. It is reasonable to deduce that he followed Newman's career with some interest, that he knew of her friendship with James Branch Cabell, and that he was aware of Mencken's respect for her criticism until her premature death in 1928.

It is even harder to say to what extent southern writers influenced him directly. Perhaps he knew of Ellen Glasgow, another friend of Cabell's, whose *Barren Ground* (1925) seems to have had a profound effect on *Tobacco Road*. The symbol of the broomsedge as a relentless natural force blindly undoing man's most painful labor dominates the first section of Miss Glasgow's novel (a section in fact entitled "Broomsedge"), just as it runs through the whole of *Tobacco Road,* achieving the same effect. It is sparks from a fire meant to destroy the encroaching broomsedge that burn down the cabin of Jeeter Lester and his wife, killing them both. Further, as the title suggests, much of *Barren Ground* is devoted to showing how outmoded farming methods abuse the soil, a theme nearly identical to that which Joseph Warren Beach calls "the chief theme of Caldwell's writing . . . the agony of the impoverished land."[27]

In sum, if we cannot precisely assign Caldwell's part in the Southern Renaissance, it is enough to observe that some of the same forces that affected the careers of such figures as Faulkner, Caroline Gordon, Allen Tate, Thomas Wolfe, and Andrew Lytle affected Caldwell too. Most simply stated, it was a confluence of experiences acting on a hitherto sheltered society that helped form these writers. Whether it was the World War, a northern or European exile, the influence of midwestern writers like Garland, Dreiser, or Anderson, or an eastern or mock-eastern college, the effect on the individual southern writer is essentially the same. He comes to look at the static world about him with new eyes. Some of these young writers discover only that orthodoxy is best after all, that fallen human nature thrives most when controlled by authority. The liberal element reached a different conclusion, like Caldwell's implicit questioning of the traditional southern way. These writers looked anew at the position of the black, the established caste system, and the privilege of the landed classes, and found the subjects they needed. In the case of Ellen Glasgow, we see a liberal mind battling with an inbred conservatism; in Faulkner, the liberalism and conservatism coalesce as he chronicles the contribution that a decadent manorial system made to a changing South.

Caldwell had seen the South at firsthand, from the dusty back roads to the city rooms of its big newspapers. He knew personally or by reputation its new writers, and he was aware of the rural American scene that Sherwood Anderson and Sinclair Lewis had opened for them. Looking about him, he saw that Anderson's poor whites had already begun to appear in Faulkner's work and that depictions of sharecroppers and tenant farmers had been done by Edith Summers Kelley, Ellen Glasgow, Elizabeth Maddox Roberts, and Harry Kroll. His work thus arises out of a rich tradition, although he is, by his own admission, not a bookish author. Because he so frequently chose southern settings; because he offers a disarming surface of naturalistic detail beneath which irony and symbolism find full play; and because he assumed a consistent point of view, concealed by bland objectivity, but constantly evoking depths of anger and protest, he may well be considered another exponent of that "symbolic naturalism" that is a prototypical mode of the Southern Renaissance. His deceiving shrug of the shoulder represents an attack on sentimentality and the legend of the Old South, all the more powerful for its apparent insouciance.

Literary Kinships

In other respects, however, he shows a kinship with a wider circle of writers. There is in many of his stories a strong proletarian strain that suggests the outlook of Dos Passos and Steinbeck. His frank, often Rabelaisian, treatment of sex owes again something to the French, something to Anderson, something to the southwestern humorous story, while his conviction that sex liberates and exalts suggests D. H. Lawrence and a zeitgeist that had welcomed both Lawrence and Joyce into the United States and would discover Henry Miller the year after *God's Little Acre.*

Early reviewers took notice of his spare prose, his "tough" attitude and the "single effect" of his stories, and compared him at once to Hemingway and the Canadian-born Morley Callaghan, just then coming into prominence. In a fit of pique, Scott Fitzgerald writing to Max Perkins called his stories "imitations of Morley Callaghan's imitations of Ernest,"[28] a revealing exaggeration that discloses some misapplied critical acumen on Fitzgerald's part. Certainly Caldwell's stories of passion and injustice often do bear a certain resemblance to Hemingway's, in that they are narrated in a modern prose style eschewing any "word that has to be looked up in a dictionary for definition and spelling"[29] and utilize a dialogue that had developed from Twain and Crane.

Triumph

At a time when Faulkner had begun to dominate the national literary scene, it was Erskine Caldwell, not Faulkner, who introduced hundred of thousands of Americans to a South about which they knew next to nothing. While the literati turned to study Faulkner, the masses read Caldwell whom they did not regard in the least as "minor" or "limited," but as tough, honest, and funny. They accepted his picture of Georgia, perhaps too literally, but in this they were not alone; so had the critics. They appreciated his bawdy humor and found his depiction of the poor white both pathetic and grimly comic. Most of all, his readers admired his courage, for here was a writer who spoke his mind, who chose subjects others never dared and wrote forcefully about them. With his emphasis on sex, injustice, the poor, and the stupid, his voice was strong, vigorous and clear. If the meaning of his stories of the dispossessed was sometimes puzzling, so then was life itself. His style, at any rate, was understandable to anyone. Caldwell, in fact, made literature available to everyone, and Americans rewarded him by purchasing his books by the millions.

Chapter Two
Caldwell's Method and World View: *Tobacco Road*

With *Tobacco Road* Erskine Caldwell found his métier and wrote the book that, together with *God's Little Acre,* would remain forever linked to his name. Abandoning the alienated "tough guys" and city settings of his earlier novels, *The Bastard* and *Poor Fool,* he presented instead a story of a Georgia backcountry family in a manner so original that it soon seized the American imagination. *Tobacco Road* is a study in outrage narrated in the studiously objective style that Caldwell would continue to use almost to the point of self-parody.

Long and rigorous training in the writing of short stories left its mark on him, he found, when he started to write *Tobacco Road.* Like Hemingway a few years before, he learned that a novel required a staying power he had yet to achieve. Unlike Hemingway, however, Caldwell was not able to make the transition flawlessly. Throughout his writing career, his novels remain brief, episodic, and dependent upon a unity of controlling themes and imagery rather than an interior coherence.

In *Tobacco Road,* Caldwell wished to treat fictionally a number of problems that interested him, some throughout his life, others particularly in the Depression years. His concern for the impoverished southern tenant farmers and sharecroppers and for the eroded soil they tilled is combined in this novel with his enduring interest in the nature of human love and sexuality, the origin of religious experience, and the mysteries of human behavior. Since his canvas is a limited one, he is often obliged to yoke his subjects, if not with violence, then in a fashion that might appear incoherent in another writer. But this disjointed, episodic narrative method is often so appropriate to his style that it invests it with a certain dignity. As a result, his stories frequently seem genuinely primitive and folkloric, although they are neither. Their rambling quality becomes an asset instead of a liability, lending them a rural southern ambience.

The Story

Essentially *Tobacco Road* is a story of the world as it should not be. Jeeter Lester, a cotton farmer who cannot afford to buy the seed and fertilizer he needs to plant a crop because of the effect of the Depression on farming in the South, lives in a ramshackle cabin with his wife Ada, whom he married as an eleven-year-old girl forty years ago. With them in squalor are his mother, a hopeless half-starved old woman who is regarded by the others as an unwelcome burden, and two of his seventeen children, Ellie May, a silent eighteen-year-old harelip, and Dude, an irrepressible sixteen-year-old boy, whose few thoughts are of automobiles and a more interesting life. The very simple plot is developed in a series of episodes and anecdotes.

A self-ordained woman evangelist from the neighborhood appears at the Lesters' to announce that God has told her to marry Dude, instruct him in the ways of the itinerant preacher, and begin an automobile crusade throughout the countryside. Jeeter, who is attracted to the woman himself and impressed by her calling, is more than willing to allow his son to marry her; and Dude, though he is repulsed by her boneless nose, accepts the proposal of a woman more than twice his age when he discovers he is to drive the new car she plans to buy. The preacher woman, Bessie Rice, is a forerunner of Semon Dye, the perverted man of God who dominates Caldwell's novel, *Journeyman*. Like Dye, like Tartuffe for that matter, she is an inspired though lecherous hypocrite, able to manipulate Jeeter by appealing to his profound, yet strangely confused religious sense. Despite her success in marrying Dude and moving into the crowded cabin, her domination over the family is short-lived. Jeeter rebels against her selfish refusal to allow him to ride in her automobile and, abetted by his wife's jealousy of Bessie, drives her and his son off their property. Several weeks later, Jeeter and Ada, alone in their cabin, are killed when it catches fire in the early hours of the morning.

Order in Disorder

Such a skeletal outline of the plot fails to do justice to its density, however, for in addition to a subplot of sorts involving Jeeter's twelve-year-old daughter, Pearl, and her husband's struggle to obtain his conjugal rights from her, there is the omnipresent account of the worn-out land and the fate of those who rely on it. In short, *Tobacco Road,* like *God's Little Acre,* consists of many stories: that of Lov Bensey and Pearl, of Dude and Bessie, of Bessie and the family, and of the family itself, all of which are told in a series of incidents and anecdotes. Yet the plot does not wander. The novel is held together, not only by the tight control of time that distinguishes much of Caldwell's writing, but also by a controlling theme and recurrent imagery. The story begins in February, the month when Georgia farmers begin preparing for their cotton crop, and ends in March, before planting has begun, though the major action covers only five days. Throughout this period, Jeeter voices his vain wish to plant cotton this spring despite his failure for the last half-dozen years. His obsession with the soil, expressed in his words and thoughts as well as by Caldwell's continual allusion to the smell of the newly turned earth and the smoke of the fires that burn off the broomsedge, constantly reminds us that the story concerns man's struggle with the earth. At the same time, a note of futility is sounded early in the book when it becomes apparent that Jeeter will again fail to plant a crop. Thus, the fertility of the spring earth is placed in ironic counterpoint with Jeeter's inability to take advantage of it.

In addition to the unity Caldwell achieves for his loosely organized novel by providing a constant reminder of the time of year and the ironic meaning of "seed time" for the character, the writer takes pains to maintain a strong sense of place. For almost half the novel, the world is viewed from the Lesters' house and yard. All entrances and exits are made in its shadow. Not only does the decaying house, crazily perched on three piles of lime-rock chips, come to symbolize the declining fortunes of its inhabitants, but it also restricts and defines the limits of their activity. The Lester tragedy is played out before the sagging cabin like a Greek drama before the façade of a temple. It is no wonder that the stage possibilities of *Tobacco Road* were so readily exploited.

Contributing further to the dramatic quality of the book is the striking device by which Caldwell opens his story. A lone figure is seen trudging two miles away from the Lesters' yard along the tobacco road, carrying a heavy turnip sack on his back. While we hear about Lov Bensey's trip to Fuller to find food, the focus shifts across the sandy ridges to what might be called a *tableau vivant.* With empty bellies, the Lesters stand in their desolate yard staring at the distant figure. Their constant bickering with one another has been briefly interrupted by a new event. Novelty of any kind serves like snuff sticks to relieve gnawing pains, both psychic and physical, they suffer. Like so many other of Caldwell's characters, they are voyeurs, lookers-on, for whom life has been reduced to the spectatorial level. Intuiting that Lov's sack contains turnips or potatoes, they stand wordlessly, scheming to take them. Lov, however, suspects their design and wishes to avoid them if he can.

But a problem has been nagging at him so relentlessly that he must seek Jeeter's help, even at the risk of his turnips. His wife, Pearl, a blonde-haired, blue-eyed child of twelve, bestowed on him in return for "some quilts and nearly a gallon of cylinder oil, besides . . . a week's pay, which was seven dollars" has refused to sleep with him or to speak to him in the year they have been married, even after he has kicked her and poured water on her. Now he feels he must get Jeeter's help, for Lov, who shovels coal all day into hoppers at the railroad chute, is not by nature a brutal man. He is, in fact, capable of deep affection for Pearl, which he periodically expresses in lyric outbursts. His mistreatment of her proceeds only from his sense of frustration. In remorse for the methods he employs to win his wife's submission, he frequently brings her presents of snuff, calico, or a "pretty" from Fuller. Exposing his sack of turnips to his predatory father-in-law is a risk he must take. Meanwhile, Jeeter regards his son-in-law's distress only as a bargaining point for the turnips in his sack.

In the first brief chapter, with utmost economy and dramatic effect, Caldwell thus introduces the themes and images that recur in interwoven patterns throughout the book: hunger, suspicion, and the failure of men and women to find or provide love; he brings on all but one of the main characters; and he casually presents two of an almost never-ending series of "outrages." His deliberate understatement makes no less shocking the fact that the Lesters are literally starving or that in the world of *Tobacco Road* children are given into marriage.

Since it would be impossible to maintain such density of narrative exposition in subsequent chapters, Caldwell deliberately varies the rhythm by recounting with teasing slowness Jeeter's theft of the turnips and Ellie May's seduction of Lov. Both of these episodes are prolonged to produce suspense and titillation, another dramaturgical device that Caldwell uses both here and, with less effect, in other books. Broadway audiences were transfixed as the harelipped Ellie

May sidled deliberately across the sandy yard to Lov and aggressively offered herself to him, an incident which, in that less blasé decade, earned Caldwell much of his reputation as a wildly salacious writer. Apparently neither the audience nor Kirkland understood that Caldwell had the more serious purpose of demonstrating that the pathetic girl's need for Lov (love) is a rejection of her loveless family, rather than an exhibition of uncontrolled desire. In prolonging the theft of the turnips, or the seduction, or later, in stretching out over a number of chapters the mindless destruction of a new Ford automobile, Caldwell not only maintains suspense but also thematically enriches the structure of his novel. The destruction of the car, for example, symbolizes the buffets the Lesters take from an uncaring world, and the car's gradual ruin parallels theirs. Thus, though we witness no explicit sexual contacts in *Tobacco Road,* we seem constantly on the verge of one. Instinctively, Caldwell knew the old lesson of the stage: "Make 'em laugh, make 'em cry, make 'em *wait.*"

The first four chapters of *Tobacco Road* provide a vignette of the Lester family which is, in common naturalistic fashion, not so much a group of individuals as a social group typical of a time and place. Jeeter steals a sack of turnips; Dude throws a baseball against the house as he complains and whines; Ellie May apparently seduces her sister's husband; the old grandmother gathers dry sticks for the stove, hoping that a fire will cause food to appear in the house; Ada, wracked with pellagra, chews on a snuff stick she has managed to withhold from her mother-in-law and morosely studies her family. Each is wretchedly dissatisfied with his lot and hates the others. Dude's open contempt for his father and sister, Jeeter's mistreatment of his mother and neglect of his wife, demonstrate that on the tobacco road there is no love of a child for parent, spouse for spouse, brother for sister.

At this point in the narration, when the reader has first become aware of an oppressive stasis, Caldwell resorts to a favorite device, the introduction of an "exciting force" in the person of a new character. The effectiveness of these catalytic characters varies considerably. In a good novel like *God's Little Acre,* Pluto Swint adds some dimension to the narration, though Will Thompson quickly eclipses him, whereas in a weak one like *A House in the Uplands* (1946), Caldwell seems uncertain what to do with the figure after he appears. In the latter novel, Brad Harrison, who is the son of a tenant farmer and seems destined for an important role in the story, makes an abrupt reversal of character in order that the author may more conveniently dispose of him. After 1947, Caldwell grew excessively careless about plotting, and his late books abound in figures who enter his stories portentously but never fulfill their promise.

But Bessie Rice, the itinerant woman preacher of *Tobacco Road,* is a stroke of genius. Her presence is foreshadowed by Jeeter's remorse for his theft of the turnips and his expressed need for immediate divine intercession if he is either to take a load of firewood to Augusta for sale or to plant his fields with cotton. Bessie is a free-wheeling exponent of a fundamentalist religion studied in exhaustive detail in Caldwell's *Deep South* (1960), a "memory and observation" of southern religious practices. Bessie's open boast to get Jeeter "on the good side of the Lord" provides her with the moral authority to control him for much of the rest of the novel.

The Anecdotal

The tightness of the initial eight chapters of the book, those covering the first day of the story, is somewhat illusory, suggested by the dominant symbol of the house and the unities of time and place, since the conflict between Lov and Pearl has apparently been forgotten, and the fate-of-the-family plot has become subordinate to Bessie's courtship of Dude. Soon after Bessie's appearance, the plotting becomes little more than a potpourri of episodes combined with passages of wistful meditation. Caldwell had followed no plan in *The Bastard,* his first published book, in which a drifter named Gene Morgan simply wanders about taking the horrors life offers him; *Poor Fool* had exhibited a similar formlessness. But he had discovered that he could flesh out an episodic plot with anecdotes like his southern stories and Yankee yarns, illustrating those quirks of an all too fallible human nature that had attracted so much attention in the magazines. From this perspective, the first three days of *Tobacco Road* may be regarded as the "time" Jeeter Lester stole Lov's turnips, the "time" Sister Bessie came visiting and decided to marry Dude, the "day" she bought a new Ford automobile, or the "day" they all drove into Augusta and stayed in a brothel, thinking it was a hotel. In fact, every chapter after the eighth could conceivably have been written as one or more short stories.

Good examples of Caldwell's anecdotal plotting and his reliance on popular and folkloric sources can be seen in the episodic chapters that

recount the events of the second day, Dude's wedding day, just after
Bessie has come by and rousted her hesitant bridegroom. The first of
these is divided into two separate sketches: the purchase of the new
car and the application for a marriage license. Both have their roots
in the endemic jokes about country folk coming to the city, though
the town of Fuller, where the sketches are set, is hardly the big city
of typical rural humor. The salesmen manage to sell Bessie a new
Ford that exhausts her bank account to the last penny. The scenes in
the showroom depend a good deal on the sort of how-you-gonna-
keep-'em-down-on-the-farm-after-they've-seen-Paree humor that, except for ever-popular television serials, vanished after World War II.
They are replete, too, with overtones of that southwestern humor that
exploits the comic potential of physical disability. Like Mark Twain,
Caldwell is both attracted and repulsed by this kind of humor. Both
writers, we might recall, introduced harelipped girls into their novels, but showed too much compassion to capitalize fully on the situations they themselves initiated. However, Sister Bessie Rice with her
boneless nose is not granted the same immunity as the pathetic Ellie
May, and the jokes fly back and forth between the salesmen in min-
strel-show fashion: "Did you ever see a nose like that before, Harry?"
"Not when I was sober."

The succeeding chapter, though it is among the book's shortest, is
also bifurcated. Half of it is concerned with the sensation caused at
the Lesters' by the sight of the new Ford, while the remainder deals
with wedding day antics. As Robert Cantwell noticed years ago, cars
play an important role in Caldwell's stories. They seem at times, he
said, "to be possessed by evil spirits"; but more often Caldwell's employment of them just "echoes innumerable second-hand jokes in the
folklore of the nation."[1] While Cantwell's observation is accurate in
part, Caldwell seems to have borrowed from the movies of his day as
well. The "pop" strain in Caldwell is strong. Current events, southern folklore, the pulp magazines, and the daily papers—all left their
mark on his writing. When Dude, busy blowing the horn, forgets to
apply the brakes till the last moment and speeds into the Lester yard,
jolting across the ditch and nearly bouncing Bessie out of the Ford;
or when cars backfire and begin to disintegrate, as they do in his early
stories, visions of slapstick film comedies dance in the head. Caldwell's characters may not throw pies at each other—they have no pies
to throw—but they throw everything else. They batter each other,
take pratfalls, fire pistols with abandon, and jump out of windows.

For all his slapstick shenanigans, however, Caldwell sometimes seems to feel that his story is losing momentum, that his invention has flagged or he is becoming repetitious. Then an automobile trip is in order, or a new character, or even, as in *Georgia Boy,* a troupe of gypsies tumble onto the scene. He identifies life with movement, and he grows anxious when activity ceases. For this reason, the serious proletarian and reform aspects of his fiction must be intermixed—incompatibly so, W. M. Frohock claims—with bustling motion and comic interruptions. Sometimes Caldwell will quickly narrate them himself from a distant perspective, as if to hurry them along. Even then he may break in with an anecdote, as he does when he stops short in describing the dreary conditions that have caused Jeeter and Ada to make burial plans, in order to tell a story of how rats in the coffin once ate Jeeter's father's face.

In bits and pieces, we learn directly from Caldwell and within the fog-filled alembic of Jeeter's slowing mind that the Lesters were victims of a Faulknerian decline of several generations, that their land was exhausted after generations of use, first for tobacco and later for cotton. As the fertility of the land waned, Jeeter's father was forced to sell off great portions of his acreage to meet taxes, so that by the time Jeeter took possession of the much reduced "Lester Plantation," timber cuttings and further land sales could not stave off mortgage foreclosures and finally the sheriff's sale about 1907. The new owner was "Captain" John Harmon, who let Jeeter stay on as a tenant farmer, offering him credit for seed and fertilizer in return for a third of his crop. But even this arrangement failed, and about 1925 Harmon gave up farming and moved to Augusta, leaving Jeeter Lester behind as a squatter. Though the Captain made no effort to dispossess Jeeter when he went, he did cut off the credit on which Jeeter had depended to plant his yearly crop. From the end of World War I, cotton farming conditions in Georgia steadily worsened until Jeeter reached the state of utter destitution described in the story, about 1930.

Social Concerns

The Lesters' hopeless state is a fictional rendering of what Caldwell actually saw during a trip home to Wrens in 1930. In the Georgia countryside, the devastating effects of the Depression on an already sick sharecropping and tenant-farming economy resulted in a degrading and despairing poverty. He saw swollen-bellied children and met sick old people dying from hunger inside the little shacks and cabins far from the main highways. The horror of this experience he attempted to purge from his mind not only through the publication of *Tobacco Road*. In 1935 he composed his bristling tract *Tenant Farmer,* investigating more deeply the plight of men like Jeeter Lester, and in 1938, eight years after the trip that inspired the novel, he delivered a series of lectures on "Southern Tenant Farming" at the New School for Social Research in New York.

In *Tobacco Road,* Caldwell had not greatly concerned himself with answers to the agricultural dilemmas of the South. Captain John Harmon, who never appears in the pages of the novel, is described as an essentially decent man who treats Jeeter with compassion and fairness and who seems to be almost as much a victim of an antiquated system as his tenant farmer. Caldwell can only chastise him mildly for failing "to show tenants how to conform to the newer and more economical methods of modern agriculture," vaguely described as "co-operative and corporate farming."

But in his nonfiction and on the platform, he offered a number of socialist remedies guaranteed to bring him further abuse from conservative Americans: for example, unionization of farm workers, with wage scales to be determined by collective bargaining, or, even more radically, the dissolution of the large privately owned farms into agricultural collectives, or widespread land reform under which individuals would be assigned small parcels for their cultivation. These programs, he suggested, should be enacted by a federal government ready to provide simultaneously a number of transitional relief measures in the New Deal pattern.

Because of his habit of interrupting his narration with action, and because he is obliged to show in considerable detail how Jeeter personifies all desperate cotton farmers, Caldwell must constantly return to the theme of the soil and the tenant farmer. The thirteenth chapter well illustrates this habit, though the chapter is not especially typical since it is entirely devoted to the one subject. Here we are given a long, interesting retrospection full of brief dramatic flashbacks recounting Jeeter's financial difficulties. We hear again in detail of the decline of cotton farming in Georgia and the shift of the source of income from the land to day labor in the mills. Jeeter's struggle to maintain his integrity in the face of impersonal forces he cannot understand gradually assumes the dimension of a surging revolt itself, one so chaotically single-minded that it rivals the force that ultimately destroys him. He reviews for himself and for us his habitual reply to the storekeepers and bankers who urge him to abandon his unproductive land for a factory job: "I know it ain't intended for me to work in the mills. The land was where I was put at the start, and it's where I'm going to be at the end." His nostrils fill with the smell of distant fires and odor of newly turned earth, as he half dozes in the spring sun with his back pressed against the warm brick chimney. Stirrings of social protest grow dimmer as Jeeter, clearly in extremis, wracked with hunger pains and despondent, weakly drifts into reveries of spring plowing and the deep sleep, death's second self, that foreshadows his approaching end.

Love and Labor

Tobacco Road, like *God's Little Acre* after it, is chiefly concerned with two subjects: the nature of love and labor. In short, Caldwell has attempted a synthesis, if not of Freud and Marx, then at least of the subjects that had attracted them. In both books, he alternates erratically between a primitivistic trust in feeling and the soil and a starkly pessimistic determinism. In *Tobacco Road,* he offers in passing some suggestions for alleviating the difficulties of the tenant farmer—though he shows no great confidence they will be acted upon—and no solution at all for the perversion of love he sees in the world about him. In *God's Little Acre,* on the other hand, he identifies labor and sex as the highest forms of human expression and looks tentatively toward a superman who will instinctively put both forces to their best use.

Because Caldwell is neither a systematic nor a consistent thinker—as W. M. Frohock once accurately observed "his attitude towards his materials is ambiguous"[2]—he has confounded those critics who have seized upon some single aspect of his art and isolated it from the elements around it. A "foolish consistency" is something that never concerned Caldwell for a moment, and if we are to read him with understanding, we must be ready to accept contradictions and to reserve judgments. If we are not alienated by his episodic and anecdotal plotting, then his thematic fluctuations need not perplex us either. Fatalism and romantic primitivism never mix completely, even in Caldwell's turbulent Georgia.

Religious View

Tobacco Road offers what Caldwell apparently believes is the balanced picture he sought of a single place at a particular time. The group of country people he shows us are utterly baffled by the world around them, a world from which they have all but withdrawn; they live nonetheless in the faintest hope that conditions may improve. With good reason Caldwell believes hope is endemic to mankind. It is perhaps instinctual and therefore like instinct can be relied upon. In other words, his is an old-fashioned "argument from design." Instincts, he believes, are to be trusted or they would not have been implanted in man. The same holds true for hope. Of course, such an outlook demands that one acknowledge a designer, but on this point Caldwell is consistently vague. Sometimes, in *God's Little Acre,* for example, he implies that man must become his own God. He says that there is a god in man and that this god is liberated when one obeys one's feelings. If these feelings were not so often libidinous, Caldwell's position would resemble Emerson's. At other times, however, he indicates that God is utterly indifferent to man and his suffering.

Such views can hardly be called "balanced"; contradictory would be a more accurate term. Yet they reflect the unarticulated beliefs of millions, especially of Americans who saw in their own time the doctrine of self-reliance in literature replaced by those of biological and economic determinism. It is because Caldwell can so frequently appeal to the deepest emotions of his readers that he has achieved worldwide popularity. His books and stories speak for those who cannot speak for themselves. Nor can he be accused of truckling to the mentality of an uncritical readership when he concludes such a novel as *Tobacco Road* with a hint that tomorrow may be better, for Caldwell genuinely takes the long view of things. Defeat is temporary. His approval goes to the man who is true to himself in relying on his feelings and instincts; and he seems to believe that as long as the human heart exists, instinctual men will arise—reason enough to believe that some will succeed.

Caldwell's attitude toward Jeeter's longing to work his land entails an ambiguity as puzzling as any contained in the novel. Obviously, it is an enormous injustice that Jeeter cannot work, and thus, like Will Thompson of *God's Little Acre,* he cannot love. But his frantic need to till the soil has an irrational element as well. We cannot dismiss it even with the tolerant shrug that we dismiss Ty Ty Walden's foolish compulsion to find gold buried on his farm, because Jeeter's refusal to leave the earth for the relative financial security of the cotton mills is the only aspect of the man to win our total approval. Yet it is clearly absurd for him to go on believing he can grow a "bale to the acre" year after year, when he has been unable for many seasons to buy or borrow the mules, seed, and fertilizer he needs to plant his cotton. His obsession, which ignores his family's well-being, is as recognizably irrational as Ty Ty's search for gold or the heroine's urge to practice fellatio in *Gretta* (1955), to mention some of the tendencies of Caldwell's characters.

Jeeter

Jeeter is certainly an example of the "strong character of marked animal or neurotic nature" that Vernon Parrington long ago identified as typifying naturalistic fiction. In fact, he is virtually a case study in neurotic traits. His behavioral patterns are always repetitive. Like the true neurotic, he is almost incapable of taking a new direction. When he is not thinking of planting cotton, he dwells on his approaching death and his fear that he will be buried in overalls, or that his body will be left in the corn crib prior to burial, where rats may get at it as they did his father's. For months, perhaps years, he has been planning to visit his long departed son Tom, a successful cross-tie contractor in a nearby county, to ask for help. Yet each time he is ready to go, he finds an excuse to postpone the trip. He is unable to bring himself to do anything about the farm or his dilapidated house. But his lassitude exceeds laziness. It proceeds from a profound, psychic despair. Even his never varying ejaculation, "By God and by Jesus," reveals not just a hazy grasp of Christian doctrine, but an inability to react to new situations with anything more than a preconceived response.

Jeeter's obsession with the soil is presented as simultaneously a divine frenzy and a saving grace: ". . . there was one thing in his life that he tried to do with all the strength in his mind and body. That one thing was the farming of his land. There had been scarcely a moment in his life during the past six or seven years when he was not thinking about it, and trying to discover some way by which he could raise cotton." His love of the earth makes him a man of principle in

Caldwell's eyes. It marks the point where his indifference and irresponsibility end. He refuses to leave the land even to earn a living in the mills of Augusta, as many of his children have, insisting that "city ways ain't God-given." His subsequent suffering is portrayed as investing him with a Job-like dignity: "The Lord sends me every misery He can think of just to try my soul. He must be aiming to do something powerful big for me, because He sure tests me hard." To his wife's objections that city life is better than starving, Jeeter offers boundless faith in God: "God is aiming to provide for us. . . . I'm getting ready right now to receive his bounty. I expect it to come most any time now. He won't let us stay here and starve. He'll send us some snuff and rations pretty soon. I been a God-fearing man all my life, and He ain't going to let me suffer no more."

But Jeeter is a strange choice as a special servant of God. He is "angry" with his pellagra-stricken mother "because she persisted in living." And he denies her food to hasten her death, though she thwarts him by mysteriously finding sustenance—"how she did it, no one knew." His wife, toothless, emaciated, and wracked with pellagra, has wrung from him the promise she will be buried in a new dress, but "she did not trust Jeeter any too much to furnish it when the time came." Jeeter's children are no more dutiful to him than he is to his mother. They have abandoned him, sending no word where they can be found. When he finally gets a request for a small loan through to his son Tom twenty miles away, he is rebuffed. Tom's bitter message sent through Dude and Bessie is to tell his father to go to hell.

Dishonest, selfish, lecherous, and brutal, Jeeter exhibits but one trait that we can approve, an unshakeable trust in the soil. Out of that Caldwell stirs us. By the conclusion of the novel, Caldwell's approval of Jeeter and of his great faith is implicit everywhere, despite the writer's purported objectivity. Jeeter's trust that God will grant him a spring planting vindicates him fully in Caldwell's eyes and more than partially in ours. Though he is a liar, a cheat, and an exploiter of those around him, he wins our pity to the extent that he is kept from accomplishing the single thing he might do. If Jeeter could labor in the fields, Caldwell seems to say, would be better. When, in the last chapter of the book, Jeeter mounts the steps of his cabin at night and inhales the odor borne from fires burning for miles around, his determination to persevere and his lyric vision of the land banish any vestige of antipathy we feel toward him.

When the winds change direction in the night, bringing destruction to the Lester cabin, the event appears almost as a burnt offering and Jeeter as a sacrificial victim. In death he becomes an inspiration to those left behind. Bessie may vilify him and refuse to offer her prayers at his burial, but Lov has been converted to Jeeter's vision of the earth. And the irresponsible Dude steps forward to speak an epilogue: "I reckon I'll get me a mule somewhere and some seed cotton and guano, and grow me a crop of cotton this year. . . . It feels to me like it's going to be a good year for cotton. Maybe I could grow me a bale to the acre, like Pa was always talking about doing."

The apotheosis of Jeeter, indeed the note of hopeful continuity sounded by Dude, may both be questionable. We have seen earlier, for example, that Dude's hope is agriculturally unrealistic; and there is little reason to believe that Jeeter was an upstanding man even in the days when he was able to plant cotton. It is, in fact, wrong to think of him as essentially a lovable old scoundrel. On the other hand, neither is he an unqualified villain. He is a classic naturalistic victim of economic, biological, and social forces. In faintly suggesting a hopeful ending, Caldwell is both true to his belief that man will prevail and yielding to the same ideal that has so often characterized American naturalism. As Malcolm Cowley once noted, American writers of this tradition have seldom been objective toward their characters.[3] Crane's heart was with the prostitute Maggie and Dreiser's with Carrie. Caldwell pities the Lesters and defends the patriarchal Jeeter. Moreover, Caldwell belongs to that essentially American school of naturalism that so frequently trusts in reform. Like Dreiser, Caldwell looked to a brave new world of agricultural, social, and economic reform; and like Dreiser and London, he mixed homemade Marxism with mysticism. In *Tobacco Road,* the literature of *Blut und Boden* comes face to face with proletarian commitment.

Man and God

Amidst the existentialist undercurrents detectable in Caldwell's early work is an attitude that sees the world as spiritually empty. God has become the monopoly of narrow-minded, mean-spirited fundamentalists, who pretend to a special knowledge of His will. Most of Caldwell's ministers, whether the clergy of organized churches or simply self-ordained "reverends" like Sister Bessie, are meddlesome busybodies or disturbed neurotics if not downright malevolent. Jeeter's faith that God will "someday bust loose with a heap of bounty" goes unrewarded.

But Jeeter's faith is hardly Simon-pure. He is as devious about God as he is about other things. He may call God "a wise old somebody" who can't be fooled, but Jeeter also regards God as an agent of his personal retribution whose ways are conveniently like his own. When Bessie tells him that God has graciously provided Ellie May a harelip to spare her the advances of her incestuously inclined father, the relieved Jeeter, who has never gotten around to taking Ellie May to a doctor, says, "The Lord be praised . . . you sure have opened my eyes to the way of God." Further, for all his apparent piety, he is convinced that he can fool God. Bessie's presence is, in fact, meant to smooth over Jeeter's numerous transgressions in the eyes of God.

If the reader has experienced the hopeless jungles of *The Bastard* and *Poor Fool,* it comes as no surprise that Jeeter's faith is unfulfilled. What may surprise, however, is that like his obsession with the soil, it is very nearly approved by the writer. Bessie may hypocritically announce at the end of the novel: "I don't think the Lord took to Jeeter too much. . . . Jeeter must have been a powerful sinful man in his prime, because the Lord wasn't good to him like He is to me." But Caldwell's own opinion seems to be closer to that of the forgiving Lov, whose epilogue is a reply to Bessie's lack of charity: "Jeeter's dead and gone, and he won't be bothered no more by wanting to grow things in the ground. That's what he liked to do more than anything else, but somehow he never got a chance to do it much. Jeeter would lots rather grow a big crop of cotton than go to heaven."

But God is not really dead in Caldwell. Rather, He is still waiting to be born. Caldwell's attitude is never that of the village atheist, angrily chiding God for not existing. Instead, like Lov Bensey, he identifies obsession with the worship of God, seeing that man can have a direct relationship to God without the need of fallible intermediaries. In many respects, Jeeter is an Emersonian whom Caldwell blesses because, like Jeeter, he too believes that self-reliance is God-reliance. This notion, however, clad in a chrisom of romantic primitivism, finds better expression in his next published novel, *God's Little Acre.* There Caldwell attempts to supply an answer for the lack of love in the world with a new sexual ethic of unrestrained passion. To obey one's urges is a sacred duty, he says, for, as Griselda puts it, they are manifestations of "God in people." In *God's Little Acre,* Caldwell accepts, too, the Emersonian doctrine that "God incarnates himself in man." The paean to feeling and the respect accorded the irrational in *God's Little Acre* are clearly foreshadowed in *Tobacco Road,* and the unconquerable spirit of man is Caldwell's final proof of the divine vitality. In reaching this conclusion he made an important shift in thought from his two earlier novels. Moreover, though *God's Little Acre,* and especially *Tobacco Road* in the Kirkland version, often appear to be rollicking parodies of the sort of *Blut und Boden* mysticism espoused by D. H. Lawrence (much like Stella Gibbon's spoof, *Cold Comfort Farm,* in 1933), they turn out to be nothing of the kind. Neurotic obsession and mindless apathy replace peasant wisdom for pages at a time, but Caldwell invariably returns to a brand of blood-consciousness not far from the Lawrentian mode.

In addition to the aura of spiritual aridity that pervades the book, accentuating its "radical" quality, is a further existential emphasis on themes of alienation and the breakdown of communication between human beings. The greatest outrage that Caldwell can envision in this world-as-it-should-not-be is the failure of human beings to love each other, or the perversion of love.

Lovelessness

No one in the novel has affection for anyone else. The marriages of Jeeter and Ada, Bessie and Dude, and Lov and Pearl are loveless arrangements meant to serve the interests of one partner alone. Only to combat a common enemy can the Lesters briefly band together, as they do to steal Lov's turnips or to drive out Sister Bessie. For years Jeeter has abused the wife whom he married when she was a child. Like Pearl, she too would run away and refuse to talk until he successfully "broke" her of those habits. He sired illegitimate offspring on neighboring wives, and now ignores Ada's pathetic request that he promise her she will be buried in a dress more presentable than her yellow calico. His own children he treated with such neglect that, like Lizzie Belle and Clara, they preferred lives of prostitution in Augusta to staying on the farm. Ada, too, has been unfaithful to Jeeter, and Pearl's real father is the man from the North—though only North Carolina—who figures prominently in other Caldwell stories.

Pearl is meant as a character foil for Ellie May, but the contrast is ineffective because Pearl is so largely absent from the narrative and because Caldwell develops a sympathy for Ellie May that lifts her above the caricature she remains in Kirkland's play. Borrowing from

Scott, or at least Cooper, Caldwell apparently imagines Pearl, who is repulsed by her husband Lov and afraid of the dark, as a skittish, fairhaired heroine—a Pearl cast among swine. Her disgust of sex, her greater "sense than any of the Lesters," her blonde hair and delicate emotional balance, are meant to set off in relief the bestial lasciviousness of the dark-haired Ellie May. But Ellie May acquires a tragic dignity as she appears on numerous occasions silently peering from behind the chinaberry tree as a dispossessed observer of the affairs of others, or when she weeps at Jeeter's insensitive remarks about her disfigurement. She shares with Pearl and with Jeeter's ancient mother the symbolic value of silence. Only by great good fortune does she avoid a horrible end like that of the grandmother whom Dude carelessly runs over, providing the novel a scene of appalling brutality, though one narrated with masterly restraint and auctorial control. Ellie May's total alienation is avoided by flight, in the same fashion as Jeeter's other children.

In deriding Ellie May's sex drive, as he does in early chapters, and in snickering at Bessie's, Caldwell displays a personal prejudice that sexuality is degrading to women. There is a strong prudish streak in this supposedly salacious writer. Only phantasy women like Griselda of *God's Little Acre* possess a sexuality that is not demeaning.

Caldwell is, in fact, rather uncomfortable about the whole subject of sex. His most devastatingly "sexy" figures are not women at all, but men like Will Thompson and Semon Dye, who leave the Darling Jills and Grettas far behind in their erotic appetites and capacity. Perhaps his uncertainty is reflected best in the dilemma of Lov Bensey, who gives indication, especially in the play, of being physically repulsive to his wife. Adolescent admiration frequently surfaces for the aggressive male who fights for women and holds them slavishly attached to himself by virtue of his overpowering virility. But this is only one small aspect of a more comprehensive view. Caldwell, like Hemingway, may be fascinated by the submissive female and the dominating male, but he is aware that such a relationship—if it can exist in the workaday world—demands an imbalance that he vocally condemns.

In most cases, he understands, one partner simply exploits the other. A woman is fickle, as *mobile* as in any classic tale of seduction, until she has been mastered. A man, on the other hand, is drawn to a woman only because she is beautiful. The attraction is always physical; the propelling force is always that of biological determinism.

Lov married Pearl because she was lovely, and despite his open confession that "he liked Ellie May more than he did her but that he did not want to have a wife with a harelip." While Caldwell never condemns infatuation, since it is an inevitable reality—indeed, he ennobles it in *God's Little Acre*—he constantly condemns exploitation. This perversion of love finds symbolic representation in *Tobacco Road* by an adult's choice of a child as a sexual partner. Each marriage in the novel is of this kind. Though Ada is now middle-aged, she was married to Jeeter as a child; Pearl was not yet twelve when sold to Lov; and Dude, only sixteen, is less than half as old as his wife, Bessie. In resorting to such symbolic representation for the failure of love, as he had used silence as a symbol of alienation or tobacco to represent obsolete agrarianism, Caldwell makes abundantly clear to the perceptive reader how far above the artless local colorist he stands despite the evaluation of obtuse critics.

Added to the economic distress that brings out the worst in human beings, their own animalistic nature drives them to hate and to exploit each other. In most of his novels, Caldwell explores the subject of the failure of love under a variety of guises, while his characters attempt makeshift solutions to a problem that baffles both them and their author. For Jeeter Lester, who is aware that his family verges on disintegration and that enmity has replaced what he uncertainly remembers as a former harmony, the only answer is trust in God. But Jeeter's God is a casual, unreliable divinity whose ways, in addition to being mysterious, are perversely slow.

Because his characters vaguely understand that elusive human love can best be assured through marriage and the unity of the family, they are often concerned with establishing harmonious marriages. Ty Ty Walden, for example, regards the family as the single hope of man for staving off chaos. But his comprehension, like Jeeter's and others', is confused. The marriages that we witness in Caldwell's pages are the parodies of a subculture directed by values and behavior it can only mimic. Jeeter's numerous children have left him. He has lost track of his illegitimate children. Yet despite his disillusionment with matrimony, he still respects it and hopes that the institution may relieve the loveless despair that surrounds him. Since God has not yet bestowed his bounty or his attention upon them, the characters of Caldwell's novels turn to marriage, or at least sex, to provide them an outlet from the distress they suffer. They hope to find love, but because they fail so completely to understand the very ideal they seek, they are seldom successful. Thus, a succession of underprivileged teenage girls, seeking the affection denied them in their families, contract alliances in the hope that what appears to work for others, and what religion has sanctioned, will work for them. Their parents smile approvingly because they have freed themselves of a burden in a way they consider socially acceptable, because they know no other answer, and because they faintly trust that the established institution may have the power to change their fortune from dismal to tolerable.

In his first two novels and in many of his later ones, Caldwell appears almost as innocent about love as his characters. In *The Bastard, Poor Fool, A House in the Uplands* (1946), *This Very Earth* (1948) and *Gretta* (1955), more knowledgeable men and women contract unsuitable matches with as little thought as his Georgia crackers. After his brief attempt to formulate a theory of sex in *God's Little Acre,* Caldwell tacitly considered the subject as beyond human ken, and observed silently the trust the figures of his novels bestow upon sex and marriage as the source of love in a loveless world.

When Lov comes running into the Lesters' yard in the final pages of the novel to report that Pearl has finally run away, Ellie May accepts with alacrity her father's suggestion that she succeed her sister at Lov's cabin near the coal chute. Her eager acceptance detracts slightly from the dignity she has achieved in the course of the book. Caldwell errs in depicting her delight with lascivious innuendo, but even as he does so he is of two minds about the incident. Ultimately, the incident is seen as a search for love that is both meaningful and honest. Lov Bensey is a decent fellow who will not abuse her, and she will undoubtedly cherish him. Through love and marriage their lives will take on added dimension, and Ellie May will not become a prostitute as have Bessie, several of Jeeter's daughters, and now, apparently, Pearl. Amidst a few inappropriate snickers, Caldwell has given his blessing to a union where a kind of equality will exist between partners and neither will exploit the other.

The Subculture

From his earliest success, controversy raged about Caldwell's modes of characterization. In the early sixties, John M. Bradbury called "his Ty-Tys and Jeeters" "phenomenological and sentimental."[4] A decade earlier, Donald W. Heiney had dismissed them as "degenerate rustics." "Caldwell," he wrote, "attributes to them a set of fleshcreeping and depressing antics, and related the whole in the flattest manner possible without comment or emotion."[5] But such judgments are both unfair and inaccurate, although it is easy to see how they originated. The characters of Caldwell's black comedies, that is, the characters of his best short stories and novels, should be regarded as less privileged kinsmen of Sherwood Anderson's "grotesques." They are people who have become "hipped," obsessed with a single subject, and who, in many cases, have let it dominate their lives. Like Anderson's grotesques, too, they are often plagued by sexual drives that impede their perspicacity. Moreover, they are frequently of limited intelligence. For example, we are told that neither Dude nor Ellie May has much "sense," a perfectly credible deficiency when we consider that the fifteenth and sixteenth children of Jeeter are the victims not only of a precarious heredity but of worse nutrition. Caldwell seldom writes about an economic or biological elite.

In short, what he writes about in his early novels is a subculture, and his approach is in many respects ahead of his time. Unlike bourgeois European and American naturalists who studied the lower classes as their mentors studied fauna, Caldwell took a sociological approach. Sociology had been a favorite subject at the University of Virginia, and when he focused his attention on the Georgia backcountry people, he looked at them as would an amateur social scientist.

There is no attempt in the Georgia stories to classify, to measure, or to identify in the sense that informs *The Experimental Novel*. Rather, Caldwell studies his Georgians as Oscar Lewis does his New York Puerto Ricans. Here, he seems to say, are people living in our time and country who are scarcely part of us. They pay lip service to our conventions, mores, and beliefs, but they do not really accept or understand them. It is exactly their groping noncomprehension that makes them so convincing. Lewis's work, in fact, supports Caldwell's depiction of backcountry people by demonstrating the enormous psychic strain inflicted on a subculture attempting to abide by customs utterly alien to it and the behavioral aberrations produced by conforming to externally imposed standards. It is the nearly futile effort of Caldwell's crackers to imitate ways they dimly recognize as socially approved, but that utterly baffle them, that produces the simian or puppet-like quality to which so many have objected.

This mimicry accounts for much of what is viewed as Caldwell's comic sense, about which there shall be a word or two later. As grotesques of a subculture they are necessarily somewhat stylized. But their reactions and their motives are credibly presented, even if they themselves are hardly familiar figures. The very terms *grotesque* and *subculture* imply a departure from a recognized norm, and it would be unreasonable to insist on judging the characters of these novels by commonplace standards.

As has been suggested earlier, Caldwell could not identify personally with his Georgia folk and he did not seek to induce his readers to identify with them. The Lesters of *Tobacco Road* are sufficiently alien to us that, as Bertolt Brecht has said about his own characters, any "acceptance or rejection of their actions and utterances" is "conscious" rather than "unconscious."[6] Caldwell's people are undeniably foreign, and their way of speaking and acting is meant to remind us of that fact—to embody "the act of alienation." We are meant to be aware of them and their abnormalities in order that we can consciously consider their situations without any danger of empathy or identification. For this reason, the controversy that once raged about how real, how true to life, are the characters of this apparent naturalist now seems irrelevant.

In limning his characters, however, Caldwell is obliged to tread the narrow line separating caricature or parody from the serious depiction of the outlandish. Usually he is successful. He has largely avoided the crushing sense of superiority and distance that Malcolm Cowley and others have said weakens the naturalistic novel. When Sister Bessie improvises a spontaneous prayer service to get Jeeter "on the good side of the Lord," her prayers are not markedly different from the effusions of the radio revival programs still broadcast in many sections of our country, and the behavior of Caldwell's characters in general resembles that of the strange folk we daily remark in the short newspaper items provided by the wire services.

If, then, we feel superior to these fictional Georgians, it is the same superiority we feel constantly in life unless we have achieved a saintly state of humility. But Caldwell does not treat his characters with the cheap irony Cowley objects to so strongly in Sinclair Lewis, the smug superiority of the writer who "if he wants to say that a speech was dull and stupid, . . . has to call it 'the culminating glory of the dinner' and then, to make sure that we catch the point, explain that it was delivered by Mrs. Adelaide Tarr Gimmitch, 'known throughout the country as "the Unkies' Girl." ' "[7] Nor does invoked

pity, which Cowley calls the companion of irony, put "a space between ourselves and the characters in the novel" because Caldwell
aimed for an objectivity in his narration so severe that many have
mistakenly believed him pitiless and have accused him of taking a
sadistic pleasure in the mayhem that overwhelms his characters. Caldwell's people are not our people, but they are recognizably human
and we study them with interest.

However, since they are in many
ways remote because of Caldwell's carefully controlled point of view
and their own limited intellectual scope, as well as their bizarre sexual behavior, it was inevitable that Caldwell would eventually lose
interest in them and turn to other subjects.

Even before he resumed the conventionally realistic characteriza-
tions he sometimes attempted in his humorless first novels, he
showed himself on one or two occasions unable to maintain a consistent attitude toward his characters. We have seen him manifest ambiguous feelings toward Ellie May. But another, more subtle example
of auctorial indecision might be noticed in the remark made by Jeeter
when a heavy load of firewood slips off Bessie's car. Jeeter "borrows"
two plow lines from a nearby cabin where blacks live and ties the
blackjack logs on once again saying: "There ain't nothing else in the
world like plow lines and baling wire. The two together is the best
in the world to do anything with. Give me a little of both and I can
do any kind of job." This distracting paraphrase of Archimedes must
bring a smile, but more than likely at the expense of serious characterization. The naturalist like the romantic means to reveal essential
human emotion and passion where both think it can best be found—
in the common folk. If Wordsworth periodically treated his rural
people with bathetic seriousness, Caldwell sometimes approached an
opposite extreme and treated his with a demeaning humor. He found
it necessary to resist strenuously the occasional temptation to forget
that his characters are human beings, not the galvanized anthropoids
his detractors discerned, since not even his commitment to a sort of
"alienation effect" could redeem such a lapse.

Humor and Naturalism

But in the larger sense Caldwell used humor with decorous restraint. In his review of *American Earth* in 1931, Horace Gregory,
writing in the *Herald Tribune,* asserted that the humorous stories in
the collection were the best. That incontrovertible judgment might

easily be extended to cover Caldwell's whole career. Only his comic novels and stories give evidence of enduring. In fact, it is more likely that it was his departure from a comic mode than his desire to achieve ever burgeoning book sales that contributed so greatly to his critical decline. Exactly what happened is not clear. Perhaps, as Allen Tate said in an introduction to Faulkner's *Sanctuary:* "There is no common law of literature which compels a writer to get better and better, year after year." Apparently Caldwell was ambivalent about comic writing. He was never a wit or raconteur like Mark Twain, for example; and he was initially reluctant to present himself as the humorist that critics and Jack Kirkland's dramatization of *Tobacco Road* proclaimed him. Eventually he moved away from bitter comedy, even though by that time he was popularly known as among America's chief humorous writers. This decision is another of the many indications that Caldwell asserted a freedom uncharacteristic of an author who would court popularity at all costs. In rejecting the comic mode, as in asserting his belief that man is incapable of dealing with life or in challenging literary censorship with new sexual frankness, Caldwell maintained his independence. He was never unwilling to combat critic or reader alike to keep control over his writing. Those who have seen him as manipulating popular ingredients to satisfy a mass audience fail to recognize how consistently he opted for artistic integrity.

Abandoning the comic mode was perhaps as necessary as selecting other kinds of characters than Georgia backcountry people, but it weakened him artistically and led him to a disagreeable pompousness that surfaces in a number of his weakest novels. As he shifted from an emphasis on social protest, the lowest levels of society, and black humor in search of a more serious realism, Caldwell's inspiration slipped away.

Though he is not in the first rank of American humorists, his talent for comedy is nonetheless many-faceted and rich. He may lack the resources of language and rhetoric available to Mark Twain or the satirical gusto of Sinclair Lewis, but he is the accomplished master of several other comic modes. Among these is his pronounced ability to recognize how a subculture, a class permanently "below stairs," apes the behavior of its betters. Caldwell may have taken his direction here from the great English humorists, but it is more likely that he simply fitted to his poor whites the habit derisively attributed to the black of vainly attempting to arrange his affairs "just like the white folks." A stratified society, whether the pre–World War II South or Victo-

rian England, offers constant example of the lower orders slavishly
mimicking their superiors. The makeshift marriages, churches, and
political institutions of *Tobacco Road, God's Little Acre, Journeyman,*
and *Georgia Boy* are crude imitations of what Caldwell's crackers and
rednecks see around them. To these folk, appearances are what count.
Just as Jeeter blithely wires on a rusty lard can to replace the radiator
of his car because it faintly resembles a radiator, so can he accept Sister Bessie into his family because she appears to offer him an easy way
to a devout life.

Their misapplied self-reliance, their fatalism, their mindless big-
otry toward blacks are subjects so disheartening that Caldwell can
only laugh at them. But he laughs as Gide's journalist in *Imaginary
Interviews* laughed at them, "on the wrong side of [his] mouth." The
gallows or black humor of the novels provides a way by which Caldwell can introduce the intolerable and the unbearable for close in-
spection. When he wishes to condemn white injustice to the black,
he listens impassively while Dude explains how he carelessly struck
a wagon with Bessie's car, killing its driver, which evokes Jeeter's
inane comment with its echo of *Huckleberry Finn:* "Niggers will get
killed. Looks like there ain't no way to stop it."

The most horrible scene in *Tobacco Road,* the slaughter of Grandmother Lester, is not simply the gratuitous sadism that many have
found it; rather, it is an example of the blackest humor Caldwell
could invent, used for the most serious purposes. When Dude acci-
dentally runs over his grandmother with Bessie's car, Caldwell is
commenting simultaneously on America's cruel neglect of the aged,
Jeeter's vicious selfishness, and most of all on the dire need and loveless lives of his backcountry people. Moreover, it is the narrator of
the story who pityingly takes notice of the old woman's agonies, after
her son and his son-in-law have forgotten her presence. When at last
they turn casually to her mangled body, it is the narrator who notes
with bitter understatement: "she had moved several feet closer to the
house." This incident—offensive as it may be to some—like "Caldwell's best stories [has] the air of native American folk tales . . . the
ones about the traveling salesman and the farmer's daughter, the
pretty school teacher and the big boy kept after school."[8] In driving
over the wretched old woman, for example, Dude is violating the
popular oath "to walk over one's grandmother" before taking a re-
pugnant course of conduct, and going it one better! Caldwell, as we
have seen, frequently extrapolates from the southwestern and other

rural humorous traditions. He delights in tales of country stinginess and ingenuity like "The Corduroy Pants" (1931) or of one neighbor's tricking another in "Priming the Well" (1931). Like Faulkner he sees comic potential in trades, swaps, and bargains of every kind.

In his pages Caldwell mixes slapstick from contemporary popular sources, folklore, and rural humor with the neurotic obsessions of a subculture in a zany combination unsurpassed by any other American writer of his time. Yet it is the black humor that predominates in the best novels, the humor a hair's breadth from horror, that has become in retrospect the hallmark of his fiction and the element in his writing most influential upon the next generation of American authors.

Regardless of the type of humor that dominates a given short story or novel, the presence of humor at all is unusual in a naturalist. But American naturalism at the hand of Hemingway, Dos Passos, O'Neill, or most appropriately, Faulkner is sufficiently unconventional to admit Caldwell's boldest unorthodoxies. Though his early books, *The Bastard, Tobacco Road, God's Little Acre,* and *Tragic Ground,* show men victimized by sweeping forces beyond their control, and though his protagonists are "strong" or obsessed figures for whom environment and heredity play important roles, Caldwell soon abandoned such conventions and later forsook even the traditional themes of the naturalist. Before the end of World War II, he had stopped writing about the struggle with the soil and proletarian topics such as strikes and unemployment, though the power of the sexual drive and the force of racial intolerance continued to interest him.

The problems he considers in novels until *Trouble in July* are essentially those of naturalistic fiction, but his solutions, when he offers any, are essentially romantic. This urge to solve such hopeless dilemmas with romantic solutions may be endemic to American naturalism with its strong strain of crypto-reform. But even the iron-willed Marx, we must recall, has been often labeled a romantic. Is a belief in a utopian classless society based on the principles inspiring the French Revolution—a society, incidentally, that Caldwell also looks to in *God's Little Acre*—any less idealistic than Caldwell's notion that a god lurks inside of man waiting to be liberated? In short, Caldwell's beliefs regarding the dignity of labor, his half-hopeful, half-wary attitude toward sex, and most of all, his trust in the ultimate infallibility of the human heart—with a concomitant espousal of primitivism—are facets of his art that dilute and sometimes clash with the pessimism, the determinism, the clinically detached and amoral attitude toward life and toward matter that he so often takes. Like other American naturalists, Caldwell is eager to assign symbolic values to traits and compulsive instincts. But in this respect he follows not just the example of his compatriots, but that of Zola, Strindberg, Gorky, and the other European pioneers. Hunger and sex drives take on symbolic dimensions in *Tobacco Road* and *God's Little Acre*. A peephole in *Journeyman* and the weaver's trade of Will Thompson, for good or ill, assume the importance of the gilded molar that McTeague covets, Trina's miserliness, or for that matter, Silas Lapham's splendid new house in the Back Bay. But undoubtedly it is his imaginative depiction of a subculture, comprised of grotesques, characters whom he portrays from a distance but without caricaturing them, that separates him from the neutral observers of strict naturalism. Though his characters are often destroyed by their compulsions and by outside pressures, Caldwell is unwilling to abandon the nobler vision of man that somehow persists within the depths of the "troughs of Zolaism."

Chapter Three
The Dionysian Man:
God's Little Acre

Caldwell's next book, his "Maine novel," written "about a family living on an isolated back-road farm in Maine" failed to win approval at Scribner's, which held an option on his next two books. Persuaded by his agent, Max Lieber, that he could easily find a new publisher, Caldwell left Scribner's and Max Perkins for Viking Press. Another cool reception at Viking to his Maine novel persuaded him to forget the book altogether, and in May of 1932, he plunged into a new story that he was already calling *God's Little Acre*.

This new book posed none of the problems of composition he had suffered with his rejected novel. Instead, he found himself typing page after page without a single revision during the long Maine summer. In August he had finished, and he brought the typescript to New York where it was promptly accepted by his new publisher. Viking gave Caldwell a larger advance than he had ever received, and he returned to Maine. His gratification, however, was tentative and largely personal. He was still almost unknown in America. As the author of two bad, unread novels[1] and a collection of short stories, *American Earth,* that had received only mixed reviews, he must have realized that *God's Little Acre* would have to exceed the modest recognition achieved by *Tobacco Road* if his career was to continue. The year 1933, when Viking promised publication of the new novel, seemed unpropitious for a young author aspiring to fame. It would be the year that the first of the great storms would ravage the Dust Bowl and drive the Oakies to the West. Business would continue poor and President Franklin Roosevelt's New Deal programs seemed ineffectual. In Europe, fascist governments were gathering force in one country after another, and at home their admirers were already visible.

Nonetheless, *God's Little Acre* appeared in an edition of ten thousand copies. The combination of some highly favorable critical no-

tices, a noisy legal battle with the New York Society for the
Suppression of Vice in which the recent Nobel laureate, Sinclair
Lewis, and other prominent figures defended Caldwell, and ever-
growing publicity reflected from Jack Kirkland's staging of *Tobacco
Road* soon ensured the book's lively sale. In it readers found a richer
story, greater variety in locale and characters, and a more vibrant
sense of life than in *Tobacco Road*. The sexual incidents hinted at in
Tobacco Road were treated vividly in the new book. But most important, Caldwell concentrated in *God's Little Acre* all that he had to say
on subjects he had only introduced in *Tobacco Road*. In this respect,
it is his most "philosophic" novel, for within its pages are contained
most of the ideas that inform his total canon. He is, of course, not
an intellectual writer, not even to the extent that Dreiser, Hemingway, or his exact contemporary, Steinbeck, are. On the contrary, he
is neither especially well-read nor broadly cultured.[2] But there is
nonetheless a clearly discernible didactic strain to him, as there has
been to other American regionalists, ranging from Eggleston and
Garland to his debased imitator of the 1950s, Grace Metalious, a
strain that drives the minister's son to articulate his world view
through the mouths of a variety of bizarre *raisonneurs*.

The subject that Caldwell undertakes in *God's Little Acre* is nothing
less than the nature of man. If he has not aspired to justify the ways
of man to God, he has at least hoped to justify them to man himself.
He seems, moreover, to have found his most profound answer in the
outright espousal of primitivism, though even here, amidst the most
solemn paeans to feelings and the God who implanted them, he is
ready simultaneously to avow the irrationality of man and to ridicule it.

The contradiction involved in championing feeling while emphasizing man's utter inability to behave humanely can be resolved only
by resorting to the traditional romantic myth preached from Blake to
Rousseau. Caldwell must somehow show that man has been perverted
by the world about him and that restoration to a pristine condition
will also guarantee the restoration of moral conscience and perception. In *God's Little Acre,* this dubious credo is expressed by Ty Ty
Walden, when he argues: "A man can't live, feeling himself from the
inside, and listening to what the preachers say. He can't do both, but
he can do one or the other. He can live like we are made to live, and
feel himself on the inside, or he can live like the preachers say, and
be dead on the inside." The choice of the preacher as symbol of false
restraint is convenient for Caldwell—although there is no such spe-

cific character in this novel—since his other books abound in these pious scoundrels. But Ty Ty's craftily circular argument cannot conceal the fact that Caldwell both parodies primitivism and offers it as a solution for human misery.

In *God's Little Acre,* the symbolic naturalism of *Tobacco Road* often gives way to an older romantic naturalism. Like Zola, Norris, and Dreiser, Caldwell becomes seized by "correspondences," extravagant connections between the workaday world of fidelity to detail and a more soaring, lyrical vision of reality. Will Thompson's heroic struggle to liberate his fellow workers from the mill owners resembles that of Zola's Etienne Lantier, and Caldwell's expressionistic identification of mill activity with life force and with sex, a linking of the mill with a world dominated by powerful wealth and sexual urges, likewise looks back to Zola's *Germinal.* His themes, his reliance on presymbolic correspondences, and his dramatic situations confer the imaginative dimension upon his fiction manifest in those earlier naturalists. Norris, in fact, might well have found Caldwell a romantic, as vulnerable as Zola to the charges he leveled against the French writer in his brilliant critical essay "Zola as a Romantic Writer": "Reflect a moment," Norris says, "upon his choice of subject and character and episode. The Rougon-Macquart live in a world of their own; they are not of our lives any more than are the Don Juans, the Jean Valjeans, the Gil Blases, the Marmions, or the Ivanhoes. We, the bourgeois, the commonplace, the ordinary, have no part."³ Violence-ridden mill strikes, gold hunting supermen of the order of Will Thompson, and a plot in which three men contend for the favors of a voluptuous woman—these elements are indeed remote from the everyday experience of the general reader.

The Story

The sketchy plot of *God's Little Acre,* almost as episodic and anecdotal as that of *Tobacco Road,* is known to millions. Ty Ty Walden, a Georgia farmer who employs a pair of black sharecroppers, has been digging on his farm for almost fifteen years, searching for the gold he is convinced lies beneath the soil.⁴ Year after year he and his two sons excavate yawning holes, while mentally shifting about from one remote corner of the farm to another the field that Ty Ty calls "God's little acre." Ty Ty means someday to contribute the profits derived from this plot, whether from cotton, corn, or hogs, to his church. At

present, however, it supports only "beggarlice and cockleburs," since
the hunt for gold is a task that leaves little time for farming.

When Pluto Swint, an obese and sweating candidate for sheriff,
stops by to "count votes" and court Ty Ty's wayward daughter, Darling Jill, he confides to Ty Ty his belief that an albino he has seen
can "divine" the lode. Convinced that this is an opportunity worth
exploring, Ty Ty makes hasty plans to kidnap the "all-white man"
and to enlist the aid of his son-in-law, Will Thompson, in digging
for the gold that soon must be found. The remainder of the novel is
concerned mainly with Will Thompson, with his impassioned pursuit
of Griselda, Buck Walden's wife, and his leading role in the cotton
mill strike in Scottsville, South Carolina.

Commentary on the plotting of *God's Little Acre* is almost unnec-
essary, since whatever has been said about Caldwell's method in *Tobacco Road* applies as well to this novel. However, one objection raised
by contemporary reviewers of the book deserves consideration. How,
it was asked, could Caldwell have disrupted a novel that began as a
richly humorous story only to digress into a depressing account of labor unrest and murder?

Such criticism contains a grain of substance if we pay less heed to
the precipitate judgment that he has somehow despoiled his narration
and more to the fact that a certain variation in tone clearly does exist
within the book. There is indeed a vast difference between the rollicking outbursts of Ty Ty in the first chapter and the solemn still-
ness of the last ones. On the other hand, *God's Little Acre* does not
fall categorically into two distinct parts. Shifts and removals link the
urban and country scenes skillfully. In addition, Will Thompson figures in a number of scenes as broadly comic as those of Ty Ty.
Though in the final analysis he is a tragic hero, or as much a tragic
hero as a naturalistic novel may contain, his remarks and behavior
connect him to Ty Ty. His vitality and delight in life, sex, and humor join him in spirit to the patriarch who eventually becomes his
disciple. But chiefly it is the theme of proletarian struggle and the
new ethic forged by the leader of the mill workers' revolt that matters
most to us and not the outlandish goings-on at the Walden Farm,
entertaining as they may be.

The humor of the early chapters contributes not only to defining
the character of Ty Ty Walden but to sharpening our perspective on
the book's major motif, the duality of man's nature and the conflict
between reason and feeling. Indeed, from the first page Caldwell toys

playfully with the dichotomy he so keenly appreciates. We initially encounter Ty Ty Walden with his two sons, Buck and Shaw, digging on their ramshackle Georgia farm, when a section of their excavation collapses. Ty Ty explodes with rage: "Why in the pluperfect hell did that dirt have to break loose up there just when we were getting deep?" He hurls his pick against the side of the crater in anger but, we are told, this display of pique is mild for him: "There were times . . . when he was so provoked that he would pick up a stick and flail the ground with it until he dropped exhausted." Given this early insight into Ty Ty's irascibility, it is comically incongruous to find him several paragraphs later lecturing his equally discouraged sons on the virtue of patience: "The trouble with you two boys is that you ain't found the patience that I've got. . . . I've been digging in this land close on to fifteen years now, and I'm aiming to dig here fifteen more, if need be."

Moreover, Ty Ty prides himself obtusely on his "scientific" outlook, although Caldwell makes it obvious that Ty Ty knows almost nothing about the technical aspects of gold mining. Ty Ty's gold fever is an obsession with him, as growing cotton had been with Jeeter Lester. He considers himself authoritative on gold mining, although his knowledge is based upon a failure so complete that he himself has never turned up as much as a single nugget in all the years he has been searching. His "argument from authority" is, then, as ludicrous as his defense of patience or his praise of farming as a way of life, and his claim to a scientific approach to all aspects of life is permanently invalidated before the reader's eyes when he enthusiastically agrees to abduct an albino for "conjur" purposes. Fired by new hope, he urges his lackadaisical sons "to be up and doing," a limp parody of the American work ethic as Longfellow had enshrined it.

In embracing a host of contradictions within himself, Ty Ty demonstrates the interior conflict between head and heart, between reason and feeling, that he discusses later at great length. But though he seldom practices what he preaches, Ty Ty Walden is a more sympathetic character than Jeeter Lester, for Ty Ty is essentially a good man. He has little of Jeeter's capacity for vicious selfishness and cruelty to others. Because he is a better man, he wins our respect more fully than did Jeeter and serves as a more creditable spokesman for Caldwell's views. His part as patriarch and sage is open to dispute, but he contains little of the lurking hypocrisy of Jeeter Lester who pretended to the same role.

For purpose of analysis the pattern of narration in *God's Little Acre* might most conveniently be viewed as a trefoil. In this design are included the story of Will Thompson, stressing themes of a new sexual ethic and proletarian struggle; that of Ty Ty Walden, emphasizing the character of the patriarch, first as a comic figure but later as a prophet-sage concerned with harmony, love, and family unity; and finally, the story of Darling Jill, Rosamond, and Griselda, which encompasses a number of motifs. Primarily, the women serve as converts to the new morality, but their courtship by several male characters provides Caldwell opportunity for a number of episodes, some "anecdotal" and others intrinsically useful to the total plot. Of these three "stories," Will's is by far the most important because it so thoroughly interweaves the other two.

The Dionysian

With the delayed appearance of Will Thompson, long prepared for by remarks of other characters, Caldwell gives his novel the scope necessary to develop two major themes and several ancillary ones. First, he can expose the conditions under which unskilled southern labor suffered in the decades before World War II, as he had exposed the plight of the tenant farmer in *Tobacco Road;* and second, in the character of Will Thompson, he finds the vehicle to introduce several ideas he had borrowed indirectly from Friedrich Nietzsche.

Influenced perhaps by Jack London, though it is difficult to say with certainty, Caldwell found himself promoting through Will and later Ty Ty the Dionysian view of life Nietzsche had described in *The Birth of Tragedy* as well as the "will to power." The Dionysian had begun to intrigue Caldwell in *Tobacco Road,* where it appeared only as a more forceful expression of a life force or *élan vital*. In *God's Little Acre,* however, it becomes intimately linked with aggressive sexual drive. In addition, the force of passion is allied with the achievement of one's destiny through the triumph of the will. Thus, even Will Thompson's name is no accident. Like Lov Bensey's, it is a tag that helps to identify his function in the novel. After he has determined to reopen the cotton mill to Scottsville's hungry workers, in the face of whatever opposition the owners can muster, and to possess his sister-in-law, Griselda, two actions inextricably bound together in his mind and in Caldwell's, Will exclaims several times in an excited voice: "I'm as strong as God Almighty Himself."

Will is first seen drunk, striding into his cheap, factory house, where Pluto Swint and Darling Jill have been sent to fetch him. On a week-long bender, he has been running about with women, rarely returning home and then only to abuse his wife, Rosamond. Looking about uncertainly, he sees Jill and Pluto and his mood changes instantly. He forgets the shut-down mill for the moment and greets the two effusively. The impression is of a figure like Tennessee Williams's "seed-bearer"—Stanley Kowalski. "Tell me how Griselda's looking these days," he asks Darling Jill. Will is at once uninhibited, vitally male, troubled, and peculiarly vulnerable. Though he is a harem-master who controls women by the power of his personality, by his profound knowledge of them, and by their response to his self-assured virility, he is also an irresponsible little boy who stirs a maternal solicitude in them and who needs them even more than they need him. His aggression, his powerful rhetoric, and his methods of lovemaking (biting and licking) identify him as an oral personality who seeks reassurance and security from women's love. To him the inaccessible, closed mill is another woman to be overcome and won. The classic dependence of the oral personality is partially projected in Will's case into his messianic mission to save his fellow workers, a clear example of what Freudians would see as a defense against his inadequacy. But the strength he needs to carry out his self-appointed task must come through the women around him. In effect, Will Thompson's libido is put to humanitarian use, since it ultimately serves the proletarian cause in the class struggle.

Here, then, Caldwell is able to show a life of obedience to the senses as socially useful and to suggest, as Wilhelm Reich and Herbert Marcuse have, that repression of instinctual drives is destructive. In pursuing his drives and obeying the powerful animal urges that possess him, Will is not only a natural man, a Dionysian listening to the god within him, but a working-class hero seizing every weapon available to him in order that his will, identical with the will of the masses, may triumph over decadent and vicious capitalism. Later in the novel, however, we shall discover the multitude of dangers inherent in the new morality Caldwell has devised for his myth of the hero in the industrial age.

Will's subsequent remarks about the absent Griselda may be read as applying almost literally to the mill as well. He babbles about her in the same wildly uninhibited fashion that characterizes Ty Ty, vowing to seduce her. His language is without the conventional artifices of adults. It rings childishly in its direct and utter unselfconscious-ness: "I'm going to get her," he says, "so help me God! I've had my eye on her ever since she moved in the house over there. Griselda's got the sweetest pair——" His embarrassed wife cuts him short with a shocked exclamation, though his artless conviction and determina-tion have their effect on Darling Jill, whose omnipresent sensuality is aroused.

While Will has sworn to "take" Griselda, he is not about to over-look his wife's sister either. The next morning Darling Jill aggres-sively steals into his bedroom while Rosamond is away. The ensuing scene demonstrates how overpowering feeling directs the actions of the figures of the novel, but it is handled with an almost Chaucerian humor that suggests not so much degeneracy as vitality. The amorous in-laws are interrupted flagrante delicto by Rosamond, who thrashes both naked bodies with a hairbrush. Neither Darling Jill nor Will, however, shows signs of guilt or remorse. Rosamond tries to stir their consciences by reminding them of Pluto Swint, who hopes to marry Darling Jill. But that ineffectual appeal is turned back by a joke of Jill's that causes Rosamond almost to smile herself. Will's innocence is pristine: "Just once was all right, wasn't it, Rosamond?" he asks. "You've had every girl in town, once. . . .," she says. "Don't you ever stop to think how it makes me feel . . .?" Unabashed Will offers an explanation: "Maybe it's because she's a Georgia girl, Rosamond." The reason-defying inanity of this reply is Caldwellian humor at its quintessential. But Will's "logic" is catching enough to infect Rosa-mond, who attempts a response to it: "That's no excuse. . . . I'm a Georgia girl myself." Irresponsible innocence shields him from his wife's fury at this critical moment. But, emboldened by success, he defends his conduct, saying, "A girl like Darling Jill can't come around without someone getting her. She was made that way from the start." Rosamond suddenly reaches for a pearl-handled .32 and opens fire. Will's nude exit from a conveniently open window is just the sort of return to slapstick that reminds us how skillfully Caldwell can switch moods. When their scurrying master departs, the sisters dissolve in tears in each other's arms, prefiguring his final departure for the mill. On his return hours later, all is forgiven.

It is, of course, the strike that gives *God's Little Acre* the identity of a protest novel and that, coupled with the inevitable decline of the Walden family, marks it as essentially naturalistic. But Caldwell's handling of the strike is radically different from the methods of such

naturalists as Zola or even Dreiser. If a comparison is to be found, it
might be with Gerhart Hauptmann who, like Caldwell, combines
a naturalistic theme with a highly imaginative presentation in his
drama of hungry Silesian weavers in revolt, *Die Weber*. Because Caldwell preferred not to rely on careful documentation of mill conditions
or faithful depiction of workers' lives, either from reasons of personal
temperament or from desire to subordinate the strike to philosophic
ideas, he turned instead to an expressionistic portrayal throughout
much of the Horse Creek Valley chapters.

Will Thompson's devotion to the mill and the town itself are explained in poetic terms more self-conscious than those Caldwell had
ventured in *Tobacco Road* to account for Jeeter Lester's love of the soil.
Rather than concerning himself with economic determinism as one
might expect, he has almost ignored the practicalities of the strike.
We do not look into workers' homes nor hear the arguments and
counterarguments for worker action, as in *Germinal*. In preparing
Will for his role of teacher, sacrificial victim, and redeemer, Caldwell
considered it necessary to sketch in the background of labor unrest in
a highly stylized fashion. His main concern, is to show Will as a vi-
sionary, a living exponent of the Dionysian life, and an example to
those around him. The task of presenting as coherent a philosophical
system as he would ever attempt may have drained his energies. Apparently aware that he could not devote himself both to Will and the
strike in a truly epic Zolaesque manner, he revived an earlier impulse
toward poetic prose to provide a kind of symphonic context for Will's
action. The result is a curious stylistic mixture of expressionism and
realism, analogous to romantic naturalism; realistic passages are in-
terspersed with soaring expressions of mysticism and the irrational,
which must later be broadly interpreted to the reader by the half-
comprehending Griselda and the fumblingly inarticulate prophet-
raisonneur, Ty Ty Walden. Will's experience, Ty Ty finally concludes, is ineffable; the "secret of living" can only be experienced
firsthand. But Caldwell's effort to communicate Will's vision of the
mill is really not so different from those attempts of Norris, Dreiser,
or Steinbeck to overcome the limitations upon language imposed by
their avowedly scientific and objective stance.

Because the strike is treated exclusively as backdrop for the emergence of Will Thompson, it lacks the substance such a turbulent subject might have played in the novel. And yet its role in the book has
convinced many that *God's Little Acre* is primarily a proletarian novel

of the Depression era. Certainly Will is a fiery workers' spokesman, and in a series of impassioned short speeches, he presents a convincing defense of the rights of labor. When he screams out, "I'll be damned if I work nine hours a day for a dollar-ten, when those rich sons-of-bitches who own the mill ride up and down the Valley in five thousand dollar automobiles," we are reminded of protest fiction. But Caldwell is not content with such speeches. He seeks to explore Will's passionate love of the mill in poetic, personal terms. Labor frees his spirit; the lint-filled air that brings on respiratory diseases fills him with delight, as does the throbbing machinery with its implicit sexual overtones: "He remembered the time when the mill down below was running night and day. The men who worked in the mill looked tired and worn, but the girls were in love with the looms and the spindles and the flying lint. The wild-eyed girls on the inside of the ivy-walled mill looked like potted plants in bloom." The identification of the machines with life force and with sex is part of Caldwell's attempt to link the microcosm of the mill with the world at large, which he sees dominated by powerful sexual urges.

Will's attitude toward the mill emerges from a series of anguished passages expressed in a style Caldwell had developed as early as *The Sacrilege of Alan Kent.* [5] A host of disjointed impressions is left to convey its own meaning, as Caldwell swiftly narrates history from a point of view almost indistinguishable from Will's own. One such passage, with discernible influences of Sherwood Anderson, from the seventh chapter, just before Will reluctantly leaves Scottsville to assist Ty Ty, typifies the tone of this section:

Up and down the Valley lay the company towns and the ivy-walled cotton mills and the firm-bodied girls with eyes like morning-glories and the men stood on the hot streets looking at each other while they spat their lungs into the deep yellow dust of Carolina. He knew he could never get away from the blue-lighted mills at night and the bloody-lipped men on the streets and the unrest of the company towns. Nothing could drag him away from there now. He might go away and stay a while, but he would be restless and unhappy until he could return. He had to stay there and help his friends find some means of living. The mill streets could not exist without him; he had to stay there and walk on them and watch the sun set on the mill at night and rise on it in the morning. In the mill streets of the Valley towns the breasts of girls were firm and erect. The cloth they wove under the blue lights clothed their bodies, but beneath the covering the motions of erect breasts were like the quick movements of hands in unrest. In the Valley towns beauty was begging, and the hunger of strong men was like the whimpering of beaten women.

Here the materialistic world of $1.10 a day has given way to a host of conflicting images reflecting the disturbed state of Will's soul and an ambivalent *Hass-liebe* toward mill life. Our minds may be full of questions: Why are the girls flourishing in the mills? Why do the men beat them? Why does "beauty" go "begging"? Why does Will, stirred by his vivid fantasies, suddenly cry out to Darling Jill: "For God's sake don't ever come over here and work in a mill." Still the gist is clear. Caldwell is deliberately antirealistic, though in a fashion perhaps more familiar to the general reader than the alienation effect he brought to *Tobacco Road*. He describes mill activity in erotic terms. The life force that pulsates in the mills is essentially sexual as was the current that vibrated through the mines of the Pas de Calais in *Germinal*. But Caldwell abandons this style before ending the first Scottsville episode in the book, and the penultimate conclusion of the section finds Will briefly arguing with a fellow worker against the AFL, which he sees as too conciliatory toward ownership, in behalf of his own radical solution of "turning on the power" and letting the workers run their own mill. Even here, however, a distant recollection of Etienne Lantier's defense of collectivism against the compromises of his rival Rasseneur might stir the memory.

It is hard to say exactly to whom the three chapters "belong" that describe the events that occur after Will, Pluto, Rosamond, and Darling Jill have recrossed the Savannah River back into Georgia. But certainly in them the center of interest shifts away from Will for the time being. Instead, Caldwell concerns himself with social criticism, sexuality, and racism. Ty Ty and his sons have successfully captured the albino, Dave Dawson, and the old man is eager to narrate in loving detail the recent adventure. More than ever he is convinced a gold strike is at hand. Finally Dave is brought in at gunpoint, guarded by Uncle Felix, one of Ty Ty's two neglected black sharecroppers. The whole family gawks at the "all-white man" in a scene so grotesque that we might wonder why Caldwell introduced it if there was not a hint that he meant it as a parody of racism, since Dave's peculiar treatment is accorded him solely on account of the color of his skin. And Ty Ty blurts out: "I can't see what an albino has got business marrying for. . . . I hate to see a white woman taking up with a coal-black darky, and this [Dave's being married] was just about as bad, because he is an all-white man."

Although Caldwell carries his satire no farther, it seems apparent that he partially identified himself with the big milky-skinned, fair-headed outcast, who, like a black, remains outside the normal pattern of life. The albino is different, too, an outsider from the swamps, whose skin and habits condemn him to the mean status of the black. Darling Jill's unconcealed interest in the boy, which ends with a tryst in the dark, is a foreshadowing of the interracial sexual adventures that other flighty Caldwellian female characters will engage in. From Dorene's seduction of Hardy in *Journeyman,* Caldwell's next novel with Viking, the theme of the black man as sexual victim of the white woman figures prominently in Caldwell's books.

Darling Jill's excitement leads Ty Ty to a few remarks on the inevitability of human sexuality. His approval of the force proceeds from an instinctive trust that it, too, must be divine. In a moment Ty Ty is expatiating on female beauty, using Griselda as a visual aid, while Dave and Darling Jill exchange passionate glances: "There ain't a man alive who's ever seen a finer-looking pair of rising beauties as she's got. Why, man alive! They're that pretty it makes me feel sometime like getting right down on my hands and knees like these old hound dogs you see chasing after a flowing bitch. You just ache to get down and lick something. That's the way, and it's God's own truth as He would tell it Himself if He could talk like the rest of us."

However, Ty Ty's subsequent elaborations on the joys of voyeurism make him sound more like a senile lecher than an apostle of primitivism or the natural life: "You're sitting there in the yard somewhere all calm and pleased and all of a sudden you'll get a notion in your head. . . . It's that old feeling again, and you know you can't stop it now to save your soul. You can sit there all day long, till it's squeezed almost to death, but it won't leave you. And that's when you go stepping around the house trying to see something. Man alive!" When Griselda tries to cut him short, he replies, "You just don't know how I'm praising you in my talk. I'm saying the finest things a man can say about a woman. When a man gets that ache to get right down on his hands and knees and lick—well, girl, it just makes a man."

This episode, combined as it is with the appearance of the albino, is so bizarre and comically vulgar that it is difficult to regard it seriously. Women are, after all, not the same as "flowing bitches," and Ty Ty's nearly incestuous interest in his daughter-in-law, together with Darling Jill's infatuation for the "all-white man," suggests that indiscriminate lasciviousness and sexual novelty are being passed off as ennobling and liberating forces. Some minutes later when Ty Ty comes upon Darling Jill and Dave coupled in the darkness outside the house, we may smile tolerantly to discover that he does not recognize what they are doing, let alone his part in inspiring them. But when Rosamond and Griselda lead Will and the puzzled senior citizen away, the mood that hangs in the air is—as Mencken described the music of Richard Strauss—"Old Home Week in Gommorah."

Will's already keen lust for Griselda is undoubtedly fired by Ty Ty's intemperate discourse, just as that of Jim Leslie, Ty Ty's absent third son, will be after a similar harangue in a later chapter. In any event, the cause of family unity can hardly be furthered by Ty Ty's indiscriminate promotion of his daughter-in-law's physical charms. On the next day Will quarrels violently with Shaw and Griselda's husband, Buck, and decides to return to Scottsville. As a mill worker he cannot conceal his contempt for the two "clodhoppers," and their contemptuous epithet for him, "linthead," disturbs him only because it is they who use it. In fact, Will takes pride in being a "linthead." For him "the sight of bare land, cultivated and fallow, with never a factory or a mill to be seen made him a little sick in the stomach." He is perfectly adapted to his place in time, a man who thrives on the choking air of the mill and the backbreaking labor at the loom.[6] Will loves the hum of machinery and delights in the bolts of printed cotton cloth that pile up from busy activity. He longs to work again, and much of this novel like *Tobacco Road* concerns itself with a Calvinist concern for the frustration felt by men denied their calling by selfish economic interests.

In later novels, Caldwell would write so often of lazy men like Clay Horey of *Journeyman*, Jeff McCurtain of *Trouble in July* (1940), or Chism Crockett of *This Very Earth* (1948) that his very name became associated with shiftless degenerates whose lives are spent avoiding labor. But his two best books accord work the high honor it had generally achieved in American letters. Work not only frees the spirit but it advances the race to the godlike state almost achieved by Will

Thompson in his novel. Writing some years later of dispossessed
sharecroppers in *The Grapes of Wrath,* Steinbeck makes much the
same identification between man and his work that Caldwell did:
"Muscles and mind aching to grow, to work, to create . . . the last
clear definite function of man—muscles aching to work, minds aching to create beyond the single need—this is man."[7]

The fifteenth chapter, marking the return to Horsecreek Valley and
the start of Will's "transfiguration," is undoubtedly the most important in the book and demonstrates, among other things, the predom-
inant place of the Dionysian theme in the novel. Scottsville continues
to be treated in the expressionistic terms Caldwell reserves to suggest
the ineffable, though how well this device works in a largely nonex-
perimental work remains open to question. We are told, for example,
that Griselda is excited by her very contact with the town. Her feeling proceeds not just from a change of scenery—though that too is
suggested—but from an awareness that dynamic forces are present
everywhere about her: "Here in Scottsville there was a murmuring
mass of humanity, always on the verge of filling the air with a con-
certed shout." Much of this tension is apparently due to the strike
that has been running for months in this tightly knit community of
mill workers and their dependents, but much is also vaguely associated with a mysterious and collective life force. Thus when Griselda
hears noises in the night, "a woman's laughter, a child's excited cry,
and the faint gurgle of a waterfall somewhere below," she experiences
"a feeling in the air of living people just like herself."[8] The presence
of a world about her makes her heart beat faster, and she becomes
aware for the first time that its people are "as real as she herself was
at that moment."

Her conclusion is simultaneously a projection of her own mental
state on others, as well as a recognition that all life—and certainly all
social strife—is a collective effort of the masses. Here, Caldwell bows
briefly toward the Freudian theory of the unconscious and the Marxist
view of class conflict, again momentarily bringing together the most
influential currents of twentieth-century thought. But the result of
this unification is cloudy, for Griselda's newly aroused sensitivity to
the world drives her only to Will. When he returns home after being
gone most of the afternoon, she longs to embrace him because "he
was one of the persons she had felt in the night air." As a charismatic
labor leader, Will is indeed a spokesman for the living people of the

night, but Griselda's attraction to him is more than philanthropic.
On the other hand, neither can it be called overtly sexual. She wants
to serve him and to mother him because "there was a painful plea in
his eyes, a look that she had seen wounded animals have."
The union local has agreed to arbitrate, a sellout in Will's eyes and
a step he cannot accept. "To hell with the damn local. . . . We're
going to turn the power on," he cries. Though disheartened by the
news he has learned, Will, too, is in a state of intense excitement as
feverish and ambiguous as Griselda's. Until now he has been suffering
a psychic impotency brought about by the shutting of the mill.
Drinking bouts and indiscriminate promiscuity have done nothing to
relieve his distress. We are not to suppose that his life is essentially
one of sexual indulgence—though that forms part of it—but rather
one of joy in labor which he associates with love and freedom. For
him as for Goethe and for Faust, whom he resembles in a number of
ways, *die Arbeit macht frei*. Will continues to think and speak of the
cotton mill in images suggestive of those ideals. While Griselda and
Rosamond stand by, Will presses shut his eyes and sinks into
thoughts of the mill narrated by Caldwell, but almost as a stream of
consciousness, full of by now familiar images and symbols and almost
a copy of the passage cited earlier in this chapter:

He could see, dimly at first, the mills in the Valley. And while he looked,
everything was as bright as day. He could see, since the time he could first
remember, the faces of the wild-eyed girls like morning-glories in the mill
windows. They stood there looking out at him, their bodies firm and their
breasts erect, year after year since he could first remember being alive. And
out in the streets in front of the mills stood bloody-lipped men, his friends
and brothers, spitting their lungs into the yellow dust of Carolina. Up and
down the Valley he could see them, count them, call them by their names.
He knew them; he had always known them. The men stood in the streets
watching the ivy-covered mills. Some of them were running night and day,
under blinding blue lights; some of them were closed, barred against the
people who starved in the yellow company houses. And then the whole Valley was filled with the people who suddenly sprang up. There again were
the girls with eyes like morning-glories and breasts so erect, running into
the ivy-covered mills; and out in the street, day and night, stood his friends
and brothers, looking, and spitting their lungs into the yellow dust at their
feet. Somebody turned to speak to him, and through his parted lips issued
blood instead of words.

Horse Creek Valley men resent their women, who can more easily find mill jobs because they accept lower wages. Throughout the Valley hundreds of "lintheads" are unemployed, though nowhere is the situation so bad as in Scottsville—Caldwell's fictional rendering of the notorious Gastonia, North Carolina—where both men and women have been locked out in an effort by management to break the strike and cut their wages. Although they are determined to win the struggle, the men of Scottsville, like Will, remember their working days with a wild pleasure. Even though the mill destroys them, they enjoy its activity. It sharpens their senses as they work in constant apprehension of early death from brown lung. The quoted passage attempts to convey the feverish excitement and sexual stimulation they feel in the cotton mill. Circuitous and expressionistic as it is, it is salted with oblique allusions to the deleterious effects of industrialization on country people. Popular beliefs regarding the mixing of sexes in confined areas, the overstimulated sexual urge of the consumptive, and the chaos caused the neurological system by night work are obliquely suggested. But the rural life, the primitivism that Ty Ty formally endorses, is largely dismissed as anachronistic. The modern man is a heroic consumptive, pouring out his energies on the night shift in a throbbing nightmare mill that never closes. Will suddenly compares the pitch of excitement engendered by this life to the state of a rabbit in its death throes: "Have you ever shot a rabbit," Will asks Pluto, "and gone and picked him up, and when you lifted him in your hand felt his heart pounding—like, God, I don't know what! Have you?"

The Death of the Messiah

Will's undisputed mastery of the little group stirs Griselda, Caldwell's epitome of the eternal female, submissive and nourishing, with a vague yearning to serve the new master. Will repeats his boast that he is "strong as God Almighty Himself" and promises to invade the mill the next day: "I'm going up to that door and rip it to pieces like it was a window shade." Despite the violent affirmation, we recognize righteous indignation. It is only the moneylenders who shall be punished. And the Christlike aura that surrounds Will amidst his female disciples is strengthened by his vow to maintain a vigil through the night. Before his sacrificial death the next day, he will suffer an agony in the garden: "To hell with sleep! I'm not going to sleep now, or any time tonight." Pluto Swint can only play the role of a terrified apostle who wishes "to be able to get up and leave." Griselda, on the other hand, sits before Will "looking up at him as if he were a precious idol come to life. She felt like getting down on the floor in front of him and throwing her arms around his knees and begging for the laying of his hand on her head." Mary hath chosen that good part which shall not be taken away from her.

The source of Will's strength for the ordeal lies not in silent prayer, however. Rather he turns to Griselda, ignoring Darling Jill's shrill warnings that Buck will certainly seek vengeance. Alluding indirectly to his future prophet, Ty Ty, Will announces solemnly: "I'm going to look at you like God intended you to be seen. I'm going to rip every piece of those things off you in a minute." And Will is as good as his word. In a moment Griselda stands naked amidst the shredded remnants of her clothes, "the most beautiful woman God ever made . . . so God damn pretty, a man would have to get down on his hands and knees and lick something." While Darling Jill, aroused to "savage excitement" looks on, Will drives an unresisting Griselda from the room to perform—albeit offstage—the first act of cunnilingus in serious American literature.

This passage, more than anything else Caldwell had written, drove the New York Society for the Suppression of Vice to call the book "obscene, lewd, lascivious, filthy, indecent, and disgusting"; and countless local jurisdictions, including the Massachusetts Supreme Court nearly two decades later, sustained that judgment. Today it still possesses power, but of a lessened sort. Perhaps it is too patently a dramatization of a common fantasy to shock. Will's ironic allusion to his ripping and shredding as the negation of his trade, and Caldwell's reminders that in shredding the cloth to lint Will "had *worked* as he had never done before," may even strike the contemporary reader as labored. Nonetheless, its religious solemnity evokes a response. If the conquest of Griselda is less shocking today to a generation of readers nurtured on stronger fare, the episode still makes an important contribution to our understanding of the informative ideas of *God's Little Acre*. Not only did Caldwell believe that he had something meaningful enough to say about sexual passion to defy the censor, but he arranged the carefully adumbrated scene to serve as a focal point for the remainder of the novel, since the concluding chapters are almost entirely dependent upon the memory of Will as the dead hero whose daring morality and martyrdom bring Ty Ty Walden from primitivism almost to Dionysianism. In possessing Griselda, Will "had acted . . . with the guidance of his want." His act was natural and hence right, though decidedly in opposition to Ty Ty's ideals of primitivism and family harmony. For although Ty Ty endorses the primacy of feeling, his primitivism is of that pastoral variety that demands fidelity on the part of nubile maidens and their swains, once the wooing is over. Ty Ty, in fact, seeks to establish order over unruly human nature through pastoral primitivism. His tolerance toward Darling Jill's sexual forays proceeds from the confidence that his daughter is rehearsing for a wifely role. Once she is married to Pluto, however, he expects her to change her ways.

How, then, can Will's dangerous behavior be justified in our minds or in Ty Ty's? The answer Caldwell provides to this question may be difficult to accept, but it is easy to discover. Will is the man worthy of Griselda. He is exempt from standards of conventional morality. In contrast to Griselda's husband, Will is a natural man who inspires submissive love in women, even the willingness to die for him, and who has knowledge of the "mystery of life" denied to Buck. Will's apparent lechery, unlike that of Ty Ty's wealthy son in Augusta, Jim Leslie, is really the manifestation of the god in man. Though many of these ideas find their fullest articulation only after Will's death, they are carefully foreshadowed in the scenes after Griselda's ravishment.

First, Griselda accepts Will's attentions in a state of quiet reverence; then, too, she is wordlessly pardoned on the next morning by Rosamond, whose reaction is in stark contrast to the display of indignation exhibited when she discovered her husband's infidelity with Darling Jill. Moreover, it is not just Griselda who in intimacy with Will "put on his knowledge with his power," like Yeats's Leda, but all three women in differing degrees. After Will's act with Griselda, the women are marked by a new composure and awareness of sisterhood. Rosamond's face is "beautiful to behold," and even the tempestuous Darling Jill is content to kiss Will's fingers while he strokes her hair in gentle preoccupation. At breakfast the three hover about him, preparing his meal "easily, lovingly." Like acolytes serving their master, "Darling Jill brought a plate, a cup, and a saucer. Griselda brought a knife, a spoon, and a fork. Rosamond filled a glass with water."

As he eats this ceremonial meal, a mood of calm fills the house. In Griselda's responsive love and the submissive devotion of Darling Jill and Rosamond, Will has found the strength he needs for the task ahead. His passion spent, his need to boast of divine invincibility gone, he single-mindedly contemplates his return to the "ivy-walled mill." When at last he leaves to meet his death in the morning, at the head of a long procession in which the three women modestly follow at the rear, he marches forth as a composite of Christ and Dionysius.

The invasion of the mill by the weavers of Scottsville is occasion for a return to the expressionistic imagery that Caldwell had already used several times. The "wild-eyed girls" with "erect breasts," who in happier times look forth from the mill's windows "like morning-glories," reappear. But this decorative touch does not detract from the power of the scene, for Caldwell shows he can handle a cast of hundreds with a skill reminiscent of Zola or perhaps epic films of the day: "Windows on the first floor were being tilted open. The crowd of women and children could follow the advance of the men by watching the opening of the mill windows one after another." Amidst the confusion comes the ominous word the company has hired extra guards from the Piedmont, alien soldiers who will slay the leader of the people. But first Will's garments must be distributed. Coming briefly to a window, he removes his shirt, tears it into shreds, and throws the ball of ripped cloth below, where women and girls scramble for the relics in a scene that looks back to the conquest of Griselda. Then a shout goes up that the power is on. Griselda's voice is heard yelling: "Will did it! It was Will!" just before a muffled fusillade breaks out from within the mill. The episode draws to an end with a death march of weavers and an appended illustration of a newly responsible Darling Jill comforting Pluto Swint, who is afraid to close his eyes for the night in this violent town.

Apotheosis and Aftermath

The concluding three chapters of *God's Little Acre,* set once again at the Walden farm, offer both an interpretation of the life of Will Thompson and a culmination to the relentless tragedy begun by

Will's possession of Griselda. Though Will is now dead this final section cannot be said to exclude him, since it is as much his as it is the girls' or Ty Ty's. The espousal of the natural life in the last three chapters by Ty Ty, or what might better be called at this point "primitivism-imposed-on-Dionysianism," reveals itself as not simply the view of a fictional character, but Caldwell's own.

Although Ty Ty had grown impatient with Will's quarrelsome ways and with his rejection of pastoralism, the news of his death reconciles him at once to his son-in-law's contrary behavior and induces a sense of great foreboding. He mentally moves "God's little acre" to its "rightful place" in a gesture meant to show his repentance for any previous hypocrisy, and turns his attention to Griselda's halting justification of Will's conquest and cunnilingus. She starts by noting the similarity between Ty Ty and Will, "the only two men I've ever known who treated me as I liked to be treated." No liberationist, Griselda reveals herself unashamedly a male sex object. She calls Ty Ty and Will "real men" and admits that she has cherished Ty Ty's impromptu declarations "about what a man would do when he saw me." Will, she explains, has actually performed the act that Ty Ty always said her beauty must inspire. "After a woman has that done to her once . . . she's never the same again." Though her logic may be faulty, Griselda seems at this point in her defense to be speaking not only of the act of cunnilingus itself but the whole ceremonial rite she has undergone at Will's hands. Ty Ty's response is to pat her hand tenderly because now "beside him sat a woman who knew as he did a secret of living." While he is gratified that Griselda's consciousness has been expanded, he has dreadful misgivings that she can continue married life with Buck. Hoping halfheartedly that Buck will achieve with maturer years the wisdom he attributes to Will, Ty Ty asks Griselda to help her husband and to teach him. But Griselda who has a few moments earlier identified ecstatic passion with the "God in people" cannot be optimistic: "He'll never learn. . . . A man has to be born that way at the start."

It is difficult to overlook the circular reasoning that characterizes Will as Dionysian because of his sexual dynamism and then attributes his dynamism to his Dionysianism. And there is undoubtedly something immature in a world view that demands woman be a submissive animal permanently cowed by a potent lover. But none of these thoughts finds expression. Instead, Ty Ty proceeds to identify the "God inside of a body" with God in general, and to argue that what pleases one must please the other. In a rambling fashion, he explains to his sons how a natural reverence allows him a pantheistic vision of the world, and concludes his homily by reminding Buck to trust God to tell him how to act with Griselda, always remembering that "if there's anything in the world He's crazy about, it's seeing a man and woman fools about each other."

The constant homage paid Will's memory by Ty Ty and the women, together with Ty Ty's discouraging insistence that his boys cannot hope to fathom Will's deeper knowledge, stirs bitter resentment from Buck. More irascible and less tolerant than his brother Shaw, Buck accuses his wife and Darling Jill of attempting to conceal their lechery with high-sounding phrases and makeshift pieties. With an inborn skepticism that cannot be shaken by his father or the women, he denies Will's vision, and becomes in his denial a Pentheus-figure, scoffing sacrilegiously at sacred Dionysian mysteries he cannot begin to grasp. Excluded in his disbelief from the circle of initiates, he vanishes to the woods depressed and resentful, as evening draws down on the day after Will's death.

At this point in his narration, Caldwell is under mounting pressure to hurry his episodic story to its violent conclusion. With great technical skill, he manages in the remaining brief chapters to provide an expanding justification for the actions taken in life by Will Thompson, an interpretation of the life of the hero for the reader and those characters of the story (like Buck and Shaw) who still do not comprehend its significance; to increase the oppressive sense of foreboding that will end in more gunfire; and to bring together and conclude what has been called here the "story" of the girls and of Ty Ty himself. This last task is accomplished mainly by assigning passages of dialogue to the old man in which he speaks at length of the primacy of feeling, first obliquely eulogizing Will, but gradually moving to themes of family unity and the need for love, themes familiar from *Tobacco Road*. Though his comments on feeling are not genuinely profound, his moral earnestness and obvious goodwill lend him authority, and he assumes characteristics of sage and prophet as he urges his family to become more charitable, more Will-like—at least "Will-like" as Will's memory is now enshrined in Ty Ty's mind. "God didn't put us here to scrap and fight each other all the time," he concludes. "If we don't have a little more love for each other, one of these days there's going to be deep sorrow in my heart." But neither does Caldwell wholly turn his back on the Ty Ty whose comic dimension has been carefully developed throughout the book. In the midst of his sermon, Ty Ty pauses to deliver an irrational defense of his search for gold, against some reasonable criticism an informed on-looker has offered. The old man's foolish insistence that "nearly fif-teen years" of fruitless experience prove lode hunting superior to placer prospecting—though neither method would likely yield re-sults—is purely emotional, instinctual, and, most important, wrong.

The "story" of the girls until now has been largely a series of an-ecdotal episodes, some humorous, as when Darling Jill steals Pluto's car or rewards Pluto for his incipient voyeurism with a faceful of soapsuds; some solemn, like the conquest of Griselda; and some melo-dramatic, as when Jim Leslie, Ty Ty's wealthy cotton-broker son, en-flamed by passion during a visit paid him by Ty Ty to borrow money, tears open the front of Griselda's dress. Now their "story" moves away from exclusive plot interest and merges with Ty Ty's, as they become converts to the vision he has derived from the life of Will Thompson. Griselda's presence, however, remains the catalyst for one last bloody episode involving Jim Leslie.

It might be argued that it is a weakness of the novel for its climax to depend upon the actions of a minor character. But Jim Leslie's at-tempt to abduct Griselda, which ultimately provokes both his own death at Buck's hands and Buck's apparent suicide, is anticipated by Will's infatuation with Griselda. In other words, it becomes a *donné* of the novel that every powerful male must be smitten with Griselda just as men were by Faulkner's Eula Varner. Though Jim Leslie is an unconvincing character in other respects, living as he does in a fash-ionable neighborhood of Augusta, married to a syphilitic, remote from his family, he is a true Walden when it comes to elemental pas-sion. This third victim of Griselda's beauty—and Caldwell's love-struck are as much "victims" as any Petrarchan lovers—is a selfish, brutal man whose passion serves no greater purpose than the gratifi-cation of his own senses, and hence we must suppose he is undeserv-ing of Griselda. But if he is as flat a character as Caldwell ever drew, his wooden presence is largely stylized, meant only to serve as a foil to Will's charismatic personality. Snob, slum landlord, and unrepen-tant capitalist, his mysterious rise to success has been achieved by ig-noring the class from which he came and by taking a symbolically diseased wife. He is an anti-Will whose lust is not a sign of vitality but degeneracy. He represents those economic forces that would not only deny the proletariat's material needs but its sexual needs as well.

Caldwell's attitude toward sex is, of course, ambiguous and must not always be accepted literally. Like Thoreau, whose term *poetic truth* comes to mind, Caldwell relies not on immediate logic to express his ideas but on the spirit and cumulative effect of the illustrations he provides. James Korges has observed that "just as the farm produces neither cotton nor gold . . . so no woman in the novel is pregnant, despite all the sexuality."[9] In short Caldwell shows us sexuality abused. Instead of being a bond between man and woman, it is a cause of hostility; instead of fostering new life, it becomes another symbol of sterility. Yet it is difficult wholly to accept such a conclusion in view of the role we have seen Caldwell assign Will. His sexual drive is ultimately approved by all the "knowing" characters of the novel. Indeed, sex was the force that liberated Will and from which he derived his energy and will to power. Therefore, it would seem either that Caldwell is guilty of a serious inconsistency or that we must regard sexual appetite in the novel as representative of all the forces over which man has little or no control. Darling Jill is unable to restrain her nymphomania because God went "too far" in her creation as her father, Ty Ty, says. Nor can Will observe conventional morality if he is to function according to his passionate nature. Human beings are the victims of their chemistry, as Dreiser had already insisted or, more simply, as Clay Horey in *Journeyman* states: "There ain't no way in heaven or hell of stopping what's bound to be."[10] Seen from this perspective, the sexuality of *God's Little Acre* is perhaps just as bleakly sterile as Korges acknowledges, but it subserves the greater theme of naturalistic determinism.

At daybreak, when Buck has not returned from the woods, Ty Ty grows anxious. While outlining the day's digging program, he finds himself obliged to explain to his black sharecroppers, Uncle Felix and Black Sam, what has happened to Will because he sees that they are aware something is wrong and "he knew it was useless to try to lie to Negroes. They always knew." He tells them how "excited about it" the girls have grown and how he has "had a hard time trying to calm them down." The blacks, Caldwell's manifest representatives of natural men, are franker in assuming Ty Ty's metaphor: "I sure reckon you do have a hard time trying to do that, boss. It's pretty hard to calm the women folks down after the male man's gone," Black Sam says. (This, incidentally, was the same year Caldwell had told the earthy southern yarn, "Meddlesome Jack," in his collection *We Are the Living* about a mean jackass whose unmistakable virility took

powerful effect not only on excited mares but had "a powerful way of
fretting the womenfolks"—black and white—so that his owner
longed to be rid of him.) Ty Ty is slightly irritated that the black
men show immediate insight into the source of Will's strength and
"the secret of living." (In *Journeyman,* his next novel, Caldwell would
demonstrate his growing conviction that the black is superior to the
white man because he is more attuned to feeling.)

At his departure, Black Sam and Uncle Felix discuss the events
that have occurred in the fashion of a Greek tragic chorus. Exchang-
ing questions with each other in broad dialect, they supply formal-
ized responses as if synopsizing the action of the story for an invisible
audience. Their perspicacity precludes any hostility to the employer
who has so often ignored their needs and reflects an understanding of
human nature indistinguishable from that Ty Ty has only recently
achieved. As they talk, these simple men demonstrate the truth of Ty
Ty's conviction that blacks cannot be duped, and reveal themselves as
apostles of the primitivism that Ty Ty has unsuccessfully tried to establish in his family. Their language grows more pointedly poetic,
until all pretense of a realistic prose style vanishes and their role becomes exclusively dramatic:

> "I was born unlucky."
>
> "Ain't it the truth!"
>
> "Trouble in the house."
>
> "Lord, Lord!"
>
> "One man's dead."
>
> "And trouble in the house."
>
> "The male man's gone."
>
> "He can't prick them no more."
>
> "Lord, Lord!"
>
> "Trouble in the house."
>
> "My mammy was a darky——"
>
> "My daddy was too——"
>
> "That white girl's frisky——"
>
> "Good Lord, what to do——"
>
> "Lord, Lord!"
>
> "The time ain't long."

"Somebody shot the male man."

"He can't prick them no more."

"And trouble in the house."

Their exchange is partially broken off as Ty Ty reappears, but they continue to mutter disjointed phrases under their breath, as if possessed, trying Ty Ty's very limited patience. Their choric *stasima* has been of such intensity, however, that no reader can fail to see that more horrors lie ahead.

At this point, Ty Ty catches sight of Buck slowly returning to the farm, and warns the blacks to say nothing to him about his peculiar disappearance. He is hopeful that Buck can be returned to digging, and in time he will forget what has occurred between his wife and Will. But in the next moment an expensive car is seen approaching the house at great speed. Inside is Jim Leslie, come to seize Griselda. But neither Buck nor his brother Shaw will allow Jim Leslie to abduct her simply because he is rich and powerful. In this penultimate scene of the novel, Jim Leslie reveals himself in the grotesque terms of *Tobacco Road*. He is an outside force, all the more threatening because of his deliberate repudiation of his family, allied to the wealthy cotton interests that destroyed Will and deprived the mill workers. His disregard of Griselda's abhorrence of him—in stark contrast to her attraction for Will—manifests his insensitivity to feeling and his willingness to disrupt the family unity sacred to Ty Ty. After a protracted struggle in which Ty Ty and all three sons exchange blows, Buck—still enraged by the betrayal of his wife to Will—fires both barrels of a shotgun at his older brother, who dies trying to reach his car.

In the confused aftermath of the killing, Buck is briefly reconciled to Griselda, who embraces and kisses him since his instinctive, violent defense of his mate has raised him to the manhood of Will. Ty Ty, shaken by the spilling of blood on his soil, blames God for putting men "in the bodies of animals" and expecting them "to act like people." But then he rejects that view. It is not God's fault, he decides a moment later, but men who do not listen to the God within them: "God made pretty girls and He made men, and there was enough to go around. When you try to take a woman or a man and hold him off all for yourself, there ain't going to be nothing but trouble and sorrow the rest of your days." Almost despondent, he turns from his family to a nearby hole to dig distractedly, while Buck, unnoticed, drifts off to the woods, shotgun in hand, to take his life before the sheriff can arrive. Ty Ty's last thought is to wonder when Shaw will come to join him in the work. Like *Tobacco Road*, the conclusion of *God's Little Acre* is a puzzling combination of darkest nihilism and faintest hope. For every optimistic sign offered, there lurks a doubly strong portent of ill. The book purports to say something of how men should live, trusting their feeling, loving, and knowing that self-reliance is God-reliance. But in Ty Ty Walden's world, a man's responses to his inner urgings lead more often to adultery and bloodshed than to oneness with God. All Ty Ty's efforts to resolve the contradiction are in vain. Human nature remains an enigma. When he returns to his hole to wait for Shaw, he is not so much hopefully cultivating his garden as indulging an irrational obsession. Only the memory of Will's character and courage survives the chaos of the tragic finish; yet he, a mixture of Dionysius and Christ, is as ambiguous a character as ever graced an American book.

Chapter Four

The Landscape of Hell:
Journeyman

With a boisterous and generally favorable reception for *God's Little Acre* from critics and general readers alike, and with the continuing success of the dramatic version of *Tobacco Road,* Caldwell realized that rural Georgia was the scene he could handle best. Since Augustus Longstreet, Georgia had lacked a voice. Now it had one that all America was recognizing, though hardly with universal approbation. Columbia Teachers College, for example, announced that it would not shelve *God's Little Acre* or *Tobacco Road* in its library, and the mayor of Chicago declared *Tobacco Road* on the boards too strong for his constituents.

But Caldwell did not seem overly concerned about these matters in his press interviews. He was thinking now of writing on an aspect of southern life he had known from childhood, fundamentalist religion. His father had frequently discussed the subject and taken his son to a variety of religious services (including the Jewish), as well as to revival and gospel meetings, in order that he might witness a full range of styles of worship. For his next novel, Caldwell decided that he would not merely introduce a preacher, as he had with Bessie in *Tobacco Road;* rather, the preacher would be a central figure who would be depicted practicing his calling. He would embody the charisma of the sort of man Caldwell had often observed in the South, one who could manipulate people and exhort them into frenzy. But like certain political figures abroad in the world, he would actually believe what he taught and would himself be invariably the maddest, most frenzied, and possessed listener of his own words. Caldwell visualized this preacher as a kind of antithesis to Will Thompson, strong and charismatic, but a force of evil, a man who did not love, whose vitality was entirely nihilistic. Instead of leading the masses, he would betray them; instead of dying for his people, he would try to kill them; instead of being a Dionysiac, he would be as spiritually impotent as his name, Semon Dye (semen die, also perhaps, demon).

In making his choice Caldwell was not only influenced by the popular approval of *Tobacco Road* and *God's Little Acre,* but probably by the earlier success of Sinclair Lewis with *Elmer Gantry* (1927) and America's fascination with the likes of Aimee Semple McPherson—a figure whose name Caldwell borrowed apparently for *Miss Mamma Aimee* (1967). Rascally preachers, especially rascally southern preachers, have worked their effect on the American imagination since colonial times. The nature of his subject probably impelled him toward the sensationalism he had largely purged from his work. Caldwell had already written his *Sanctuary* when he wrote *The Bastard* and *Poor Fool,* but now the tendency to introduce episodes of gratuitous violence crept back into his writing. Because he was enormously busy both as a writer and an elusive celebrity, Caldwell sought further inspiration for his new novel in the rich deposit of his short stories, a practice he has sometimes used during his long career. Thus, his "August Afternoon," published a year or two before in the fall 1933 first showpiece issue of *Esquire,*[1] provided the nucleus for *Journeyman.*

Short Story Genesis

Here it might be appropriate to briefly survey Caldwell's stories before examining "August Afternoon" as the source for *Journeyman,* for by 1935 Caldwell had already published three collections of stories, representing nearly half his total output in this genre. Caldwell's early stories are without question his best, although like so much of his work, they are remarkably uneven. His vignettes of Depression hardships make melodramatic reading today. Many of his stories of young love or sexual awakening are sentimental, bathetic, and clumsily written. Nevertheless, it is to the early collections that we must look, not only for his most enduring work, but for the origins of the techniques he brought to his novels.

By his own admission, Caldwell is a storyteller who tends to think of the short story in terms of the southern oral tradition. He believes that the short story, like all literature, should "improve upon nature." This critical concept helps us to understand his constant bewilderment at being labeled a naturalist, for his own professed critical theory is often romantic. He tries to entertain and to provide heightened emotional experience for his reader—to leave him, as he once said, "physically reeling and emotionally groggy." Moreover, his trust in oral literature drives him to imitate the storytelling practices of the South, personified in his mind by the whoppers his grandfather allegedly told. A characteristic remark of Caldwell's is the one that serves as an introduction to "Autumn Courtship" in the collection *Jackpot:* "I believe this story would have been far superior if it could have been told orally."[2]

His stories depend upon the same anecdotal technique that characterizes his novels. Rather than with "once upon a time," they start: "Nothing much ever happened in the upper part of Pine County until Lem Johnson went over into the next county and married a swell-looking girl named Ozzie Hall" (523); or "Nobody could ever explain exactly why it was, but the girls who lived in all the other parts of Oconee County were different from the ones in our section" (135). This narrative method evokes a sense of the past that simultaneously bestows dignity on the tale and excites the reader's interest. They have such titles as "Where the Girls Were Different," "Memorandum," "The Lonely Day," and "It Happened Like This." They invariably begin in the past tense: "Hod Sheperd was in the kitchen eating breakfast when he heard one of the colored boys yell for him" (3); or "Back in January, about the middle of the first week, Ned Jones received a letter from the fire insurance agent's office in Bangor" (339). Moreover, this mood of recollection allows the writer certain liberties in dealing with facts.

Then, too, they are often episodic, or at least as episodic as the short fiction genre allows. In writing "My Old Man," a story that grew into *Georgia Boy*, Caldwell claimed: "I read the first part of this story and immediately wrote the second. Afterwards I went back and read the first part for the second time, and straightway wrote the third part. By now the reader may wonder why I did not write a fourth part. The reason is, simply, that I did not read it again" (193). Even in such a tightly written story as his splendid "Midsummer Passion," Caldwell approaches the climax of the story slowly. We read in detail how Ben Hackett was prepared for his erotic misadventure with Mrs. Fred Williams by finding a pair of pink panties and a jug of hard cider in an empty automobile on a country road after a day of haying. Ostensibly, Caldwell could have stopped here, playing off Yankee industry against frivolous sexual fantasies, but he takes it a step farther when Ben suddenly attacks Mrs. Williams, a long-time neighbor, in her garden. His mission is a panty-raid in reverse. He wants to place the pink panties he carries in his pocket upon Mrs. Williams.

Characters like Ben Hackett are closely related to Jeeter Lester and Ty Ty Walden. They are obsessed men, grotesques in the manner of Sherwood Anderson, whose private visions of the "truth" blind them to the world around them. Whether Yankees or southerners, they are victims of *idées fixes,* by which they measure all events in their lives. Sometimes they are eccentrics like Max Clough, who cannot abide women until his neighbor Elam Stairs acquires one for his farm. Sometimes their obsessions are more dangerous. For example, hatred of the black inspires many of the most vicious characters in both his long and his short fiction.

Some of his funniest stories are tales of hoodwinking in which one neighbor tries to outsmart another, a kind of yarn enshrined in American regional literature. Typically a farmer tries to bamboozle his wife or a neighbor. His Yankee figures are often motivated by an overdeveloped sense of thrift or Down East shrewdness, such as Jake Marks who takes a nude bride to obtain full advantage of an obscure "shift marriage" statute absolving a new husband of responsibility for his wife's bad debts; or his southerners are frequently out to show their neighbors and the world the breadth of their vision or the depth of their lust. His themes often remind us of Faulkner, for Faulkner also writes of swapping services, trades, lynchings, hunting excursions, burial wishes, country people mistaking brothels for rooming houses, and miscegenation. Caldwell's stories, like Faulkner's, feature Indians, woodsmen, and corpses that resist burying, and bear the same close resemblance to his novels that Faulkner's do.

"August Afternoon"

"August Afternoon" is an almost unknown story of Caldwell's that exemplifies many of these characteristics of method and theme. It is a superior story, one of Caldwell's best, which not only foreshadows the plot of *Journeyman* but exhibits a lifelong concern of Caldwell's writing, the problem of keeping a woman. As "August Afternoon" tells us, women are by nature slight creatures who are nevertheless drawn to powerful virility. In fact, it is the mystique of the male that concerns Caldwell far more than that of the female in his best work. Darling Jill may have been the sexiest heroine in American fiction up to Caldwell's time, but she herself was hopelessly captivated by Will Thompson's overwhelming sexuality. In Caldwell's view, men must fight like sled dogs to hold their mates against splendid outsiders, an attitude often expressed earlier in the work of Jack London. This interest in the effect of dazzling virility upon women is apparent even in Caldwell's earliest novels. However, he often depicts the sexually exciting male as a dangerous, even psychotic figure who usually carries a knife or revolver and is totally amoral. Even Will Thompson, of *God's Little Acre,* the most attractive of the lot, is nearly mad. The cuckolded husbands, on the other hand, are often ineffectual, even comic characters.

Such a character is Vic Glover, protagonist of "August Afternoon," whom we first meet coming out of a deep sleep, Caldwell's recurrent symbol for escape from reality. The heat of the noon rings in Vic's ears, the heat that is so often a precondition for violence or irrationality in Caldwell's stories, for he imagines the baking sun reduces men and women to their essential, fallible natures. Though *Tobacco Road* is set in February and March, such novels as *God's Little Acre, Journeyman, Trouble in July, Georgia Boy,* and a host of short stories, including "Saturday Afternoon" (1930), "Savannah River Payday" (1931), "Memorandum" (1931), "The Medicine Man" (1933), and "Meddlesome Jack" (1933), depend upon the scenario of hot weather and the symbolism that Caldwell extrapolates from it.

Vic Glover is another one of those rural grotesques whom credulous critics once regarded as absolutely faithful depictions of real life. Like Clay Horey of *Journeyman* he has married a teenage wife, and is now faced with the problem of holding her. He is awakened to danger by Hubert, his self-effacing and deliberately stupid black tenant farmer, who has just noticed a white stranger lurking about. Since Hubert carefully avoids any uncomfortable situation that might arise between Vic Glover and the stranger, it is odd that he should warn his irascible employer. His behavior may be attributed both to the constant desire of Caldwell's characters for novel experience and in light of the ambiguous attitude toward the black in much of his early work. He sees the black as long-suffering and humane, but still resents his protective defense of assumed ignorance, his conditioned evasiveness in answering all questions, and his willingness to see "white folks" humiliated. Hubert embodies this dichotomy since he is well aware that the stranger means trouble for Vic Glover, yet he is eager to see how Vic will react, even if it means endangering himself.

The mysterious stranger has appeared from nowhere, Hubert tells Vic, and now slouches under a water oak, whittling and gazing un-

abashedly across the glaring sandy yard at "Miss Willie" who sits on
the porch steps. Willie, moreover, seems flattered by the attention
she is receiving. Hubert several times pointedly reminds his white
boss that fifteen-year-old Willie "ain't got much on," while Caldwell
implies that the stranger's angle of vision takes maximum advantage
of that fact. The stranger, who shortly asks Willie her name and introduces himself as Floyd, represents another "exciting force," an
evolution of the figure Caldwell had introduced in both *Tobacco Road*
and *God's Little Acre*. Floyd serves as the prototype of Semon Dye, the
menacing itinerant preacher who suddenly appears at the Horey farm
in *Journeyman*.

Like Will Thompson, Floyd (and Semon Dye) demonstrates what
appear to be Dionysian qualities, though these inspire no praise in
"August Afternoon" or *Journeyman*. The difference is that Will was a
great teacher-labor leader, whose attraction for women was not simply the thoughtless pursuit of the childless male for sexual gratification. The figurative language of *God's Little Acre* was designed to
articulate the significant lesson of Will's life: the superman's will is
stronger than any interior inhibition, just as it is stronger than any
outside social repression. Will drew on the power derived from sexual
mastery to free the proletariat, to achieve a more perfect liberation
than either Marx or Freud had foreseen. Semon Dye, on the other
hand, frees no one. Instead he enslaves Clay Horey whose name (clay
and whorey) is as unflattering and appropriate a tag as Dye's. Nor has
the preacher any discernible philanthropic mission in life, certainly
nothing rivaling Will Thompson's need to reopen the mill and "turn
on the power."

After vainly sending Hubert to learn the stranger's business, Vic's
decision is to confront Floyd with a "steel yard" in his hand; but before he can raise himself to his feet, Floyd draws from his trousers a
long switchblade and begins silently toying with it: "It was about ten
or eleven inches long, and both sides of the handle were covered with
hairy cowhide" (33). One need not be a seeker of esoteric symbols to
recognize the phallic implications of the long steel blade jutting out
from its hairy hilt. The sight of the knife, or on another level, the
recognition of the superior sexual force of the charismatic stranger,
causes Vic to back down. Instead he remains where he is and orders
Hubert to take away Floyd's knife. Hubert very sensibly refuses, despite Vic's bullying. Although he loses no opportunity to remind Vic

of his incipient cuckoldry, the black man plays dumb and impotent as Vic attempts to shift to him his own responsibility:

> "Have you got a gun, Hubert?"
> "No, sir, boss," Hubert said.
> "Why haven't you?" he said. "Right when I need a gun, you haven't got it. Why don't you keep a gun?" (37)

Subsequent threats to Hubert are of no avail.

In the meantime, Willie has submitted to caresses and kisses from Floyd and been persuaded to forsake the hot steps for a sylvan glade some distance from the house, where a well is found. In this clearly mythological setting, the Dionysian stranger from the north (Carolina, actually) takes his pleasure with the nymph while Vic "listened to the sounds that were coming from the pine grove" (38).[3] The third person anecdotal account of an August afternoon ends with Vic setting Hubert on watch to notify him when the lovers return and then sinking back into oblivious sleep.

For a variety of reasons, the story is a good example of Caldwell's early work. It is by no means an artless country tale. While one would have to search long to find a traditional plot in the oblique narration, it is obviously constructed of the same materials as his novels and depends much upon the same techniques, especially, those of *God's Little Acre* published the same year. The mythic impact is neither realistic nor at all what we have been led to associate with Caldwell. The theme of male sexual anxiety is suggested from several directions, only one of which I have indicated, and is supported by a complicated web of images wherein Freudian and mythological symbols are major strands.

In such elements as the repetition of phrases from Hubert (We ain't aiming to have no trouble today, is we?), an "exciting force," and southern humor, Caldwell has exploited the same methods he used effectively in his longer prose narratives. Indeed, "August Afternoon" shows conclusively that Caldwell's stories served as trying grounds for his novels and in this case specifically for *Journeyman.*

Journeyman

In revising his short story into a novel about a fraudulent preacher's backcountry revival, Caldwell was obliged to alter and greatly expand his plot, but he largely maintained the same setting. *Journeyman* offers the familiar Georgia backcountry of *Tobacco Road* and *God's Little Acre,* a region of baking heat and sandy soil, where the actions of characters are ruled by what is around them—or not around them—as much as by any interior motivation. Suffering a nearly cosmic ennui amidst the dreary surroundings they inhabit, they look with childish delight to any break in the monotonous pattern of their existence, however disruptive such an event may later prove. Though the people of *Journeyman* are not literally hungry like those of *Tobacco Road,* they are almost as poor, loveless, and starved for novelty. Here, too, teenage wives, like Clay Horey's Dene, mated to older men await a chance to escape the deadly routine of their empty lives.

To bring momentary respite to the apathy of Rocky Comfort, Georgia, there appears one day at Clay Horey's farm the gaunt, black-clad figure of a man "who looked as if he had been living on half-rations since the day he was weaned." Semon Dye, the self-ordained itinerant, or journeyman, preacher who climbs out of his overheated flivver in the hellish nimbus of "a dense cloud of nauseating black smoke" is only a confidence man. But like Melville's confidence man, he "is the agent and source of satire rather than . . . the incarnate object or victim of it."[4] Perhaps, in Caldwell's case, *satire* is not the correct term, for *Journeyman* offers little of the ridicule of characters and institutions to be found in classic satire. Yet it does offer in comic fashion a vision of a world characterized by deceit, selfishness, and greed. Like Melville's *Confidence-Man* the meaning of *Journeyman* is not always clear. Still, as R. W. B. Lewis has noticed of Faulkner's *The Hamlet* and Nathanael West's *The Day of the Locust,* *Journeyman* too displays a literary kinship with Melville's *roman noir* because it boasts a "super-promiser"—as Caldwell's friend Pep West called "the supreme tempter" who, Lewis says, prowls in these novels through the world, "assisting it towards its promised end."[5]

Journeyman is in some respects Caldwell's gloomiest and most existential novel because it concludes neither with a note of hope nor with the faint suggestion, so often a part of naturalism and Caldwell's fiction, that though an individual be destroyed the race goes on. There is no promise in this book that the entelechy of the organism will in time produce a hero. Rather, for hope, the opiate of novelty is substituted. Clay Horey wishes only that the monotony of his existence be relieved, not that his life be improved. A visit from some-

one like Semon Dye, with all the dangers it entails, is the finest event
he can imagine. Like the Lesters, whom we first witness dumbly
watching to see which way Lov Bensey will turn because they have
nothing else to do, Clay Horey and his circle solve the empty riddle
of their lives by seeking a new face, a new wife, or a novel experience.
They are content—confidence man and conned alike—to peer mind-
lessly at absolutely nothing for minutes at a time through a crack in
a cowshed wall. Tom Rhodes, Clay's neighbor, admits there is nothing to see through the hole but confesses: "I just come down here
sometimes and sit. . . . I don't have much else to do, so I just sit
and look through the crack." These folk, too, have become voyeurs
for whom idle curiosity replaces a will to live as productive human
beings, though with far less reason than the inhabitants of the tobacco road.

If we perceive that peeping through a crack in a cowshed wall—
realistically depicted as that scene is—is meant to carry a value
beyond the mere event itself, to depict a total alienation from a
meaningful life, then it is difficult not to regard the larger setting of
the novel as similarly symbolic. Indeed, in this respect *Journeyman*
looks away from the romantic naturalism so often apparent in *God's
Little Acre* to the more consistent symbolic naturalism of *Tobacco Road*.
In that book Caldwell had relied upon a deceptive simplicity of setting to achieve genuine dramatic effect and to provide silent commentary on the pathetic tragedy acted out on the sandy soil before
the Lesters' sagging cabin. Now, in *Journeyman* he attempted much
the same thing, while reviving in pristine form the grotesques of his
short fiction and of *Tobacco Road* in the persons of Clay Horey and
Semon Dye, each of whom is recognizably realistic while sufficiently
remote to embody the act of alienation. George Becker thus errs doubly when he calls such characters "ludicrous monsters, who like
Thurber's unicorn inhabit one's familiar garden, but are nonetheless
monsters for all that."[6] They are by no means monsters but neither
is the "garden" they inhabit as "familiar" as he implies. Caldwell's
setting is both an actual world and an imaginative one, where "the
grotesque alignment of particulars from the actual world . . . distinguishes the real."[7] His atmosphere is nearly always symbolic, despite
its apparent realism. When he describes the "April sun beating down
upon the magnolia leaves" in *Journeyman,* we are subtly reminded of
his early vow to rid southern literature of the scent of magnolias once
and for all. He can evoke with a quiet effect, and an eloquence to

rival Thoreau's, the insidious encroachment of nature on a neglected New England farm without a hint of the pathetic fallacy. The briars and white pine of *A Lamp for Nightfall* are nonetheless as menacing as the broomsedge in *Tobacco Road:* "Juniper was beginning to choke out the grass in the pastures; wild blackberry briars were covering the cropland; the old hayfields were already shoulder-high with gray birch; and white pine seedlings grew in every available opening."[8]

To Caldwell, southern fundamentalism of the 1920s and 1930s is another part of the southern landscape as real as a chinaberry tree and as grotesque as a chain gang.[9] Fundamentalism was a subject he never tired of, and in *Journeyman,* he found the opportunity to give it full scope for the first, though not last time, for in the late 1960s he wrote a whole book devoted to southern religion, an expanded version of one he had had published several years before in England. *Deep South* (1969) provides a respectful and affectionate "memory" of his father, the Reverend Ira Sylvester Caldwell, together with an account of a number of religious experiences the two shared, and an "observation" of the contemporary southern religious scene, written in much the same fashion as the texts he had prepared for the photo-essays written in collaboration with Margaret Bourke-White. While his impressionistic approach to cultural anthropology—an approach marked by the long unidentified quotations from anonymous observers that characterize the photo-essays—may seem random if not somewhat biased, it is impossible to read far into *Deep South* without recognizing his deep knowledge of the subject. Caldwell not only knows the usual varieties of Baptists, Methodists, and Presbyterians, but he also has a wide acquaintance with such exotic sects as Holy Rollers, Snake Handlers, Hammer Heads, and Foot Washers. Moreover, the middle ground of southern churches, largely fundamentalist and evangelical, is familiar to him as well. Nor is his knowledge creakily out of date, the observations of his early career. His remarks on Bob Jones University and the civil rights activity at "fine brick churches" black southerners often attend rather than the earlier "slab-sided shacks" with "rusty tin roofing" demonstrate that he has followed the progress of southern faith out of the Depression into the contemporary moment.

Although the focus of Caldwell's distaste for fundamentalism has shifted somewhat over the years, the elements that contribute to his strong feeling have remained consistent. First, he resents fundamentalist preachers as enemies of his swarthy father whose liberal Christian views grew more advanced in Caldwell's mind with passing years. Though Ira Sylvester, as Caldwell called his father, might have looked a bit like Semon Dye, dark, muscular, and tall in a black suit and string bow tie, he had little patience with the excesses of the type Dye represents. The elder Caldwell, like his son, believed that fundamentalist preachers manipulated the emotions of the ignorant. Ira Caldwell, a strong rationalist, shared H. L. Mencken's opinion that only the "savage" of the "gospel tent pretends to know the will and intent of God exactly and completely."[10] On the other hand, his son, sympathetic to romantic beliefs in the goodness of man and the trustworthiness of feeling, assessed the fundamentalist preacher as a superfluous, self-seeking intermediary standing between man and God.

Of course, both understood the attraction of fundamentalism to the rural and urban poor. More than a quarter of a century after *Journeyman,* Caldwell wrote in *Deep South:*

There are many reasons for the widespread popularity of fundamentalism among economically and socially underprivileged Anglo-Saxons in Southern rural regions and factory towns. A listing of them would include the folksy atmosphere of informal religious service, temporary surcease of loneliness, constant references by the minister to impending death, the promise of instant salvation, a rousing tempo of piano and guitar music, the incitement produced by detailed examples of sexual immorality in sermons, and the opportunity to indulge in emotional spasms in public without inhibition.[11]

Thus, though he hated the sin, he loved the sinner, and fundamentalist religion remained for Erskine Caldwell the most genuine expression of emotional irrationality outside the lynching or the sexual encounter and hence a worthy subject for his interested study.

Because the fundamentalist preacher could serve no real purpose in easing man's worn spirit, Caldwell came to regard him as a confidence man. Sister Bessie Rice had been the first of these frauds, a lecherous, selfish parody of the Christian minister. Caldwell probably borrowed his depiction of her insatiable sexual appetite from folkloric sources, and he saw no reasons why Semon Dye should not be equally lascivious. By 1935, sex had become Caldwell's stock-in-trade in the public mind, but in his own mind, sex served as a metaphor to express his vision of the South, just as it had for Faulkner. At the same time, in order to become more southern, he became less political. The strong proletarian sympathy expressed in *Tobacco Road* and *God's Little Acre* is altogether absent from *Journeyman.*[12] In fact, he seems

deliberately to have ignored the charge he leveled two years later in
You Have Seen Their Faces that the fundamentalist church fawningly
"conducts itself along lines calculated to give the least offense to his
[the landowner's] social, political, and economic creeds."[13]

However, fundamentalism itself plays no absolute role in this
novel. Semon Dye need not necessarily have even been a preacher.
Rather it serves as a vehicle to display and define the world of *Journeyman* and to provide Caldwell an economical means to depict the
mentality of such a world. In brief, by introducing the subject he has
taken an intellectual shortcut and saved himself much description and
explanation. *Journeyman,* he says in effect, is set in fundamentalist
country, and one knows what to expect there, inside a house, a barn,
or a man's mind.

But Semon Dye is less easy to fathom than his victims. Like the
protagonists of Caldwell's two preceding novels, he is a severely
flawed figure. But in *Journeyman,* Caldwell was faced with the dilemma of resolving strong sexual urge—the mark of the natural
man—in a largely malevolent character. Jim Leslie Walden of *God's
Little Acre* could not be mistaken for a natural man and was easily
dismissed as a lecherous force of evil. Though his sex drive resembled
Will's superficially, his rejection by Griselda, together with a host of
telltale clues, revealed that his desire was nothing more than lust. In
contrast, Will's was certain evidence of the "God in man." Now, in
Journeyman, Caldwell had to indicate clearly where the compelling Semon Dye, a figure of powerful sexual urges, ranked on the moral
scale. His answer appears to be that Dye is a fraud, one who cheats
himself even while cheating others and who is denied the final fruits
of victory because he is not pure of heart.

He survives the debacle of a botched revival meeting, a humiliat-
ing end no genuine tragic hero could endure, and leaves Rocky Comfort with the celerity of an unmasked sharper, though the episode of
his departure contains elements sufficiently ambivalent that his hasty
exit may also be read as the discreet flight of a mildly successful confidence man. Though he is a villain, he differs from Jim Leslie Walden because he believes his own words. Like Will Thompson he is an
exponent of the will to power and becomes for a short time nearly
invincible. He is genuinely convinced that he is a chosen man. But
his belief that he is exempt from conventional morality—"I'm Semon
Dye. . . . The Lord don't have to bother about me. He sort of gives
me a free rein"—reminds us not of Will Thompson, who never gave

the subject a thought, but rather of figures like James Hogg's "justified sinner" or Browning's Johannes Agricola, for he is every bit as mad as that crazed antinomian. Like Johannes Agricola, Semon Dye "knows" that he has a unique relationship with God and special dispensation relieving him of the strictures that bind others. His God-intoxication pours forth in late scenes of the novel as he attempts with all his strength to win souls for the Lord, distorted as his concept of that mission might be.

Dye cultivates a variety of vices. Like Elmer Gantry, he drinks and he gambles, but most significantly, he womanizes. Possessing a knowledge of these frail creatures to rival Will Thompson's, he appears in their eyes as a prophet filled with the spirit of God and exuding a powerful male magnetism not to be resisted. Caldwell's depiction of women in this novel is about as unflattering as he would ever achieve. As certain remarks in the Modern Library introduction to *God's Little Acre* make clear, he regards women—at least sexually experienced women—as little better than animals. Sex may or may not ennoble a man, but it always degrades a woman. Though he may joke about female sexual appetite from time to time, his laughter inevitably sneers. Ellie May is "horsing" with Lov, Dude tells his father excitedly: "That's horsing from way back yonder!" and Ty Ty implies that a woman is pretty much the same thing as "a flowing bitch," while "Meddlesome Jack" tacitly compares women to mares in their stalls, fiercely aroused by the sensed presence of a potent jackass outside the barn. The image is always animalistic. For all his daring frankness, for all his noble ambition to liberate southern writing from the genteel tradition, he remains in thralldom to that tradition. His depiction of an inspiring woman—for example, Pearl in *Tobacco Road*—is as curiously laundered and insipid as a Fenimore Cooper heroine. His salacious reputation notwithstanding, Caldwell remains more than a bit of a prude.

Lesser women than Pearl, however, long for virile men to fulfill them, charismatic males who will simply overpower them; and Dye depends on his control of women to earn an uncertain living. His initial revival meeting, for example, will begin with a service aimed at the women, in his certain knowledge that once they are won over the men will follow. When he gains a quick mastery over the women of Rocky Comfort by his commanding presence, Dye takes on Dionysian characteristics in the reader's eye. The new preacher is a stranger from the North whose legendary reputation precedes him and who insists that he is exempt from conventional morality, as he urges others to follow his daring ways. But just as he is an anti-Christ who perverts the Christian gospel of love, so is he an anti-Dionysius who offers hate and death and who is guilty of the very lewdness of which Pentheus so unjustly suspected the real god.

Nonetheless, though Dene's dull eye may gleam, as apparently do those of many local drabs, the fundamentalist preacher remains inescapably a deceiver, a "super-promiser" who provides merely a single moment of shabby eroticism to a bored and lonely teenager. For all this magnetism, his is the very limited power of the Father of Lies. Only those who cooperate with him or who offer him no resistance can be overcome. Squatting in the dirt near the chimney, loaded dice in hand, his revolver lying significantly between his legs, he is clearly a fraud, the very antithesis of the divine Dionysius. His pistol cannot match the phallic power of the god or of a godlike character like Will Thompson. Semon Dye can vanquish only nonentities like Clay Horey and then simply because Clay acquiesces in his own defeat. He accepts Dye's invitation to shoot dice and is too cowardly to defend the child-wife he exploits. Instead, he is persuaded to put her up as a stake in the game.[14] There are few men in Georgia or the world, Caldwell tells us, who will fight for their wives. In fact, in *Journeyman,* there is only one, and he is a black. The act of resistance or, in existentialist terms, the freedom to say no to wrong can raise a man to a hero, an idea Caldwell had already suggested at the end of *God's Little Acre,* when Buck was briefly reconciled to Griselda after killing her would-be abductor, Jim Leslie. In essence, Clay Horey's cuckoldry is not just a conspiracy between the potent Semon Dye and the compliant Dene. Rather, it occurs because of Clay's cowardly failure to resist evil head-on, evil he had instinctively realized from the moment the preacher alighted from his Ford. Clay permits the seduction of his wife and a variety of lesser offenses when, like Adam, he refuses to renounce the work of Satan's namesake Semon.

But the satanic preacher's will can be resisted by those of courage, even women, and Caldwell eventually chooses Lorene, Clay Horey's ex-wife, the predecessor of Dene, to teach this lesson. His attitude toward her fluctuates, however, as toward so many of his female characters; and an appreciation of her uneven characterization and her role in the story can only be achieved by a persistently faithful reader.

Lorene had left Clay and Rocky Comfort some time ago for Jacksonville, Florida, where, we learn, she has drifted into a life of prostitution. She is apparently still in love with Clay, though why is a mystery since he demonstrates few lovable qualities. Although she accepts her new career with equanimity, she has returned to Georgia to visit her son, Vearl, for whom she feels a genuine affection. It was not the city that corrupted her, however—a theme Caldwell would treat nine years later in *Tragic Ground*. Now her beauty, self-assurance in male company, and well-developed taste for corn whiskey makes her a provocative companion for Tom Rhodes and Semon Dye. Clay, on the other hand, is anxious about what detrimental effect she might have on Dene.

Clay's growing interest in Lorene and her unembarrassed admittance that she is "hustling" in Florida give Semon Dye an idea: he proposes that Lorene and he move on to Florida together after his Sunday revival meeting where he will pimp for her while still attending to the Lord's work. The team will split profits equally. Her ready acceptance suggests to Semon that their partnership might begin immediately. When Lorene dismisses Semon's choice of a first client, Tom Rhodes, the preacher suggests Clay himself. This plan is actually carried out in a subsequent chapter in an anecdotal episode, obviously owing much to popular sources, when Clay is tricked into paying Semon Dye for the sexual favors of—if not his present—at least his recent wife. But much of the broad humor of the scene goes sour when Semon Dye brutally forces Clay to consummate the union after Clay has discovered that he has been gulled. And the sex act itself is concluded with a solemn earnestness:

> "I don't reckon there's ever been anybody like us," Clay said for her to hear.
> She tried, until tears came to her eyes, to hold securely their ultimate possession.
> "It used to be like this all the time, didn't it, Clay?"
> He nodded, looking at her.
> Semon was standing over them then. He looked down upon them, urging them to leave the loft.
> "I'll be back again sometime, Clay," she promised.
> "I won't stay away always. I'll come back."

Even if these vulnerable lovers are no better than they should be, they seem enveloped at this moment in a kind of innocence. They remind us of Adam and Eve, as Semon Dye stands over them wielding a terrifying pitchfork like a Boschian fiend.

Lorene, as Semon's new partner, may appear a strange choice of an agent to withstand him. But as Caldwell progressed with her characterization, he came to see her in a new light. Instead of the irresponsible provincial prostitute he had first envisioned, she grew closer to the archetypal "whore with the heart of gold." Not only is Lorene more perceptive than Semon Dye's other victims, she is kinder. If she has long since compromised her integrity, she has not lost her soul. Semon slowly realizes the challenge she offers him, though it is little more than a faint repugnance to him, an affection toward Clay, his most willing victim, and a skepticism that could infect others. Consequently, he singles her out for special treatment, at one time delivering her a vicious pistol whipping when she comes between him and Clay. Why Lorene should still plan to leave for Jacksonville with the man who has beaten her, or why she will willingly attend his revival meeting, are questions not readily answered in the novel.[15] She must, of course, be on hand for the climactic scene of the novel, the long Sunday meeting at which Semon Dye will exhibit his vaunted preaching talents and attempt her conversion. Caldwell is careful again to keep the best for last, true to his instinctive belief that suspense is the finest weapon in the storyteller's arsenal.

By the final chapters of the brief novel, Rocky Comfort (where the sun beats "without mercy" on the sandy soil and fires burn day and night to kill the broomsedge) has become a microcosmic hell presided over by Semon Dye who even announces, "The devil is everywhere in Georgia." And his long-awaited Sunday revival meeting assumes the shape of a pandemonium. *"Radix malorum est cupiditas,"* Semon seems to say, and by that he means cupidity, not greed. Like Chaucer's pardoner, another damned soul and stirring preacher, he knows that sin vividly portrayed brings in the highest profit: "The worse sins . . . the better they like to listen," he says. By seven o'clock in the evening, his revival is ready to reach its wild climax. He is determined that everyone sitting in the schoolhouse will be "saved," and to that end he labors mightily. When Lucy Nixon starts to "come through," the meeting suddenly becomes a general exorcism, though it may well be the devil casting out devils. The gyrations of the faithful grow explicitly sexual. The noisy, confused rite is a paean to irrationality. But the feelings expressed are not pure, emanating from God who directs the uncorrupted man from within. Rather, these emotions are a mockery of the primacy of feeling. The country people have become pawns of Semon Dye, who stands between them and

God, diverting divine impulses into lascivious mockeries of true feeling. Now the whole congregation is on its feet twisting and turning voluptuously. Lucy continues to be shaken by convulsions, until her breasts, stomach, and thighs tremble uncontrollably. "Men jump about like animals," "like unruly stallions," while women shake their bodies in rhythm with Lucy: "A man who had been watching her for several minutes suddenly grasped the fly of his breeches with his fist and ran yelling into the crowd. Bursting buttons flew into the air like spitballs." Semon dashes about the one-room schoolhouse, administering to jerking, twisting, screaming bodies. Speaking in tongues, shouting ejaculations, he drives out devils left and right as one after another "comes through." Clay is soon one of these, shouting out ecstatically: "I've got religion! I've got it."

Yet it is Lorene that Semon longs to "save." As the frenzy grows, the equation between exorcism and orgasm becomes blatantly apparent, and Semon's desire to make Lorene "come through" (or more simply to "come") is nothing less than an expression of his desire to achieve sexual mastery over the woman: "Lorene," he begs, "try to come through for me now, won't you? Nearly everybody else in the schoolhouse has come through except you." But he cannot succeed. She feels only a contemptuous pity for the preacher whose self-control is beginning to slip away before her eyes. Failing several times to move Lorene, who sits calmly watching those around her in the throes of wildest emotion, Semon abandons the effort and allows himself to be carried away like the howling forms around him. "Unga-unga," he yells out, and, forgetting Lorene, gives himself up to emotion: "His face was losing its expression of pain, and a beatific smile spread over his face. A moment later he was sprawling on the floor, writhing and kicking and tearing his hair and clothes. He lay on the floor in the dirt and dust at her feet, kicking his lower limbs as though each successive movement would be his last on earth." In surrendering to his own passion it is, of course, Semon Dye who "comes," not Lorene. He has failed utterly to master her, and as he sinks to the floor in sweaty exhaustion, dully watching Lucy Nixon's ecstatic convulsions and the communal orgy reaching its throbbing climax, all thoughts of the collection he had been anticipating slip from his mind.

Caldwell's story is almost over. Nothing is left except that the mysterious stranger disappear as suddenly as he came, precisely what happens. As readers we are free to conclude that Semon Dye is only

an arrogant and careless confidence man, moving on under cover of
darkness, taking with him the memory of Dene's favors, Clay Horey's
car (lost in a dice game), and a sum of cash extorted from that cuck-
old; or, what has been suggested here, that he is a dangerous and
wicked force who vanishes in disgrace, defeated by a woman who
would not succumb to his wiles.

The visit to Rocky Comfort in that case takes on some of the dimensions of a descent into hell. Though Caldwell had apparently begun the novel only as an expansion of "August Afternoon," a more
leisurely examination of the subject of female promiscuity and the
Dionysian powers of the virile male, he soon found himself more concerned with a portrayal of the anti-Dionysian, the charismatic male
whose vigor and will resemble that of the natural man but who is as
different from him as a true minister of the gospel is from a fraudulent journeyman preacher. As the character of Semon Dye became recognizably diabolic, Caldwell decided to oppose him, not with a
courageous man, but with a woman lacking the traits he finds so offensive in most women.

Because *Journeyman* is sometimes carelessly written and contains little of the perceptive social criticism of *Tobacco Road* and *God's Little
Acre* and none of the proletarian concern these novels offer, it cannot
rank with them as a literary achievement. It does present, however,
a new and affirmative vision of the black as the true natural man, as
well as a number of passages implicitly condemning his oppression.
Much of the novel, of course, attacks irrational and exploitative
southern popular religion, making of the book an exposé, like *Tobacco
Road,* and placing it in the tradition of Zola and Norris. Moreover,
Journeyman exhibits a skillful development in imagery, an employment of a quasi-biblical symbology, and is sustained by a setting at
once realistic and suggestive.

In the last analysis, *Journeyman* would appear to be concerned with
the existence of evil and man's attitude toward it. Caldwell's tempter,
Semon Dye, vanishes, not only because Lorene successfully resists
him, but because he is a victim of his own lies. But his defeat must
be seen as limited and temporary. Lorene, indeed, expresses anger
that he has left without her; and Clay who correctly suspects that
Dene, too, hoped to leave with Semon, confesses he misses his erstwhile persecutor: "Somehow I sort of hate to see Semon go away now
and leave us. It makes me feel high and dry. I'm going to miss having him around here for a while to come. It makes me feel lonesome,

not hearing him talk and not seeing him sitting on the porch, waiting for Sunday to come." This is the gloomiest note of all, because
Clay's words are an admission that the human heart is inclined to evil
and attracted to sin. Man must indeed be depraved when he longs for
the return of the devil.

Caldwell and the Black

From every perspective, *Journeyman* provides plentiful evidence of
the evolution in attitude toward the black that Caldwell had undergone from his earliest novels. In the years after he left the South for
a predominantly northern residence, he moved fitfully from a non-
committal observation of the indignities suffered by the black man in
The Bastard, or even from an insouciant hostility toward the misce-
geneous amours of the arrogant black middleweight, Knockout Har-
ris, in *Poor Fool,* to the half-pitying, half-amused interest of the local
colorist in *Tobacco Road* and "August Afternoon." But in later work
the black comes to be a long-suffering figure of such ferocious virtue
as to be nearly unbearable. It is in the final pages of *God's Little Acre,*
however, that the best portrayal of the black as natural man occurs,
Caldwell's version of the noble savage. Here he illustrates his belief
that the black man, more attuned to feeling than the white, is poten-
tially a better man, ethically and morally. When he came to write a
new introduction for the Modern Library edition of the novel late in
1933, he expressed this opinion openly, saying "that the Negro has
yet to sink as low, economically and morally, as the white man. He
holds much the same position to the white man as the male of the
human race does to the female. No man has yet reached the depths
to which a woman can sink; and I doubt very much if the Negro will
ever fall to the lowest depths of the white race."[16]

Caldwell demonstrates the black's innate moral superiority in *Journeyman* by stressing the loving solidarity of the black family. Always
convinced that marriage and family unity is the single best hope to
stave off the chaos threatening human beings, he contrasts the affectionate marriages of two black couples with the exploitative union of
Clay Horey and his fifteen-year-old wife, Dene. Susan and George,
who live in a cabin a short distance from Clay's home, are the parents
of a "raft of pickaninnies," but Susan has nonetheless accepted Clay's
little son, Vearl (a syphilitic), into her family, feeding him, washing
his clothes, and giving him the love his father withholds. Vearl con-

sequently prefers the company of the "quarter." Here he sees loving black fathers treat their children to oranges trucked back from Florida for white employers, and Susan tucks him into her own bed while she goes about her morning chores.

Although Clay has been meaning to take Vearl into McGuffin to see a doctor, he has through sheer inertia constantly postponed the trip. In portraying Vearl as syphilitic and neglected by his parents, Caldwell is creating for his sixth novel a composite of two earlier fictional figures: Ellie May, whose father Jeeter never found the time to have her harelip treated, and the diseased little Caliban that Gene Morgan's stepsister-wife bears in *The Bastard*. In that novel, which Maurice Edgar Coindreau has seen as Caldwell's violent reaction to the genteel tradition of Edith Wharton and Willa Cather,[17] Morgan throws his syphilitic child into the river before abandoning his wife. The adoption of a tainted and neglected white child by a black surrogate mother demonstrates the black's faculty for the charitable and loving life that Caldwell enthusiastically endorses in successive novels.

Nor does he make the point in a single contrast. Rather, he returns to the subject with a variety of examples. Another black couple whose marital fidelity remains exemplary, though sorely tested, is Sugar and Hardy Walker, two of Clay's "hands." Semon Dye, intent on seducing Sugar, leads her into Clay's house, patting her on the buttocks as he walks, "stroking the wildness out." The simple mulatto girl cannot resist the malevolent power of this fundamentalist Svengali, "the potentest thing" as Dene calls him. But when Hardy—whose name is a clue—finds her missing, he runs at once to Clay's. Apologetically, but insistently, he inquires for his wife, even daring to enter uninvited through the front door, in stark defiance of southern racial taboos. Inside Semon will not relinquish Sugar to her husband, however: "Keep back, or I'll shoot you down to start with," he warns. "You can't fool with me, I know how to handle yellow niggers like you." But Hardy is not intimidated by Semon Dye, as nearly every white character of this novel is, and Dye is obliged to shoot. At the explosion Sugar falls across her husband to protect him with her own body. As Semon levels his gun menacingly for a second shot, Sugar drags her helpless, bleeding husband out of the room and away.

Clay's startled response to this scene of horror echoes in callousness Jeeter's "niggers will get killed." Peering through the settling dust and the acrid cloud of gunsmoke, he says: "I don't mind seeing a

dead darky once in a while, . . . but I sure do hate to see one of my
hands passing away on me right at this time. It's planting time, and
no other." His concern is only that Semon Dye might have killed a
field hand. "If Hardy was to die," he continues, "I'd have to get out
and do some of the work myself. I sure would hate to see him pass
on." Labor, like marriage, is accorded a special dignity in Caldwell's
novels, as we have seen earlier. Hence Clay Horey's attempt to avoid
it for a life of sloth, an ambition shared by many of Caldwell's poor
whites, must be regarded as highly reprehensible. In *Trouble in July,*
his next novel, Caldwell carefully repeats these same illustrations of
black moral superiority. At one point when a rabble-rousing night
rider urges a crowd of tenants and sharecroppers to rid the countryside of its black inhabitants, a voice from the crowd replies with brutal logic: "String one of them up ever so often. That'll make all of
them keep their place. Hell, if there wasn't no more niggers in the
country, I'd feel lost without them. Besides . . . who'll do all the
work if the niggers was sent away?"[18]

In reversing the black's popular reputation, in depicting him as an
exemplary parent, spouse, and worker rather than a shiftless, irresponsible, and wanton trifler, Caldwell introduces a radical element
into his composition of a symbolic language. The dusty country
around Andrewjones and Rocky Comfort will continue to be popu-
lated by "niggers," but they will somehow be different, more formi-
dable than they first appear.

In forsaking the proletarian sympathies of *Tobacco Road* and *God's
Little Acre,* Caldwell engaged himself in a lifelong campaign, the
championing of the black. That is not to say that the black is the
hero of *Journeyman.* Semon Dye, the villain, remains the unchallenged
protagonist. But the innate nobility of the black man, the abused pe-
ripheral figure of the southern landscape, commands our attention as
a profound moral lesson in homely virtue.

Later Caldwell would be faced with the problem of dealing with
black characters who grow ever more morally perfect. Because he had
insisted on identifying the "feeling" of the natural man so closely
with the libido, he labored under an enormous handicap. From *Journeyman* on, he sought to show that the black's popular reputation as
oversexed was an unfair one. It is Dene, we hear in her admission to
Semon Dye, her confessor-seducer, who lured Hardy into her embrace: "I let him know he could have me. He wouldn't do it then,
but I wouldn't let him go. I locked the door and wouldn't let him

out. Then I let him know that he had to. He was afraid, but I made him stay." This is a scene that Caldwell often repeats with slight variations in the years to come. How different in tone are Jeeter Lester's remarks when he worries vaguely about the fate of Ellie May after he and his wife are dead: ". . . there won't be nobody to watch after her. If she stayed here at the house by herself the niggers would haul off and come here by the dozens. The niggers would get her in no time, if she was here by herself."[19] Caldwell found himself compelled to de-sex the black to make him more acceptable to an American audience, but suffered in the process the consequence of robbing him of the vigor that constitutes the natural man.[20] In later novels, the black man becomes a neutered paragon. Caldwell grows so sensitive about depicting sexual appetite in the black that he often rejects adults for adolescents or young men. Thus both Ganus Bazemore of *A Place Called Estherville* (1949) and Jeff Bazemore of *The Weather Shelter* (1969) are mulatto youths forced into compromising situations by lustful white women, and consequently exposed to southern violence for defiance of racial taboos. Caldwell apparently gave them the same surname coincidentally, for though their characters and situations are remarkably similar, there is no indication at all that they are related. The novels, published some twenty years apart, are set in Georgia and Tennessee, respectively.

Chapter Five
Trouble in July
and *Tragic Ground*

Till the End of the War

Journeyman's critical reception was not warm, though the book would soon achieve the giant sales Caldwell's name now guaranteed. However, he had little time to concern himself with what critics were saying about the novel since this same year he also saw through the press a new short story collection, *Kneel to the Rising Sun,* a farm-reform tract, *Tenant Farmer,* and his first sociocritical travel book, *Some American People.* He was, in fact, on the verge of a period of almost frenzied production. In the next eight years, from 1936 to 1944, he managed to publish fourteen new titles while devoting himself to a startling variety of time-consuming activities ranging from long trips to the world's trouble spots, to war broadcasting from Russia, and to undertaking regular journalistic assignments. Some of the books appearing in this period—in addition to reissues of earlier works—were simply anthologies or pieces written earlier. For example, *The Sacrilege of Alan Kent,* which came out in 1936, had been written in three parts years before. Because it was published in a small private edition, the public largely ignored it, though a few critics examined the impressionistic, highly poetic work with disapproving interest as a sample of what Caldwell might have done if he had continued in that direction. *Jackpot* (1940), for which Caldwell wrote a long series of introductions, contained only nine new stories. In 1944, now represented in special Armed Forces Editions of books for soldiers, Caldwell received permission to publish a wartime book in compliance with government paper restrictions. *Stories,* edited by Henry Seidel Canby of Yale, was subtitled "twenty-four representative stories" and contained a flattering and perceptive critical foreword by that well-known man of letters. In contrast to these books, the photo-essays, prepared with his second wife, Margaret Bourke-White, required elaborate preparations and exhausting journeys to remote sections of Eastern Europe and the United States, but they were rewarded by unanimous acclaim. Not since Mathew Brady had such a talented American photographer appeared at the locations where history was being made, and Caldwell's taut understated prose fit Bourke-White's stark pictures magnificently.

In spite of dizzying schedules, he wrote four novels during this period: *Trouble in July* (1940), *All Night Long* (1942), *Georgia Boy* (1943), and *Tragic Ground* (1944). *Trouble in July* offers an account of a lynching, largely from the perspective of a timid Georgia sheriff determined to avoid any involvement lest he damage himself politically. The contemporary setting encompasses the last of the American lynching years, a period that ran from the Reconstruction until the end of World War II when in Georgia alone more than five hundred blacks lost their lives to mob justice.[1] In considering lynching and injustice to the black man, themes he had often handled in short stories, Caldwell almost found the opportunity for which he had been searching to present the black as natural man. In exhibiting him as ethically superior to his white persecutors, *Trouble in July* demonstrates a logical development of ideas enunciated clearly in *Journeyman*. But the development of this theme in the person of Sonny Clark, a black youth of scrupulous virtue lynched by a mob after being accused of molesting an empty-headed white girl, is marred by sentimental characterization that weakens the book. Despite this artistic failure, Caldwell did not abandon the theme permanently, though he put it aside for the time being.

All Night Long and *Georgia Boy*

In fact he left the southern scene altogether in a patriotic attempt to lend his pen to the Allied war effort. With *All Night Long* (1942), he vented the sentimental side of his character again. This novel of Russian partisans shows a depth of sentimentality that few had suspected existed, but which is as representative of his total work as his carefully cultivated "indifference." Although an examination of the short stories would have revealed a deeply ingrained bathetic streak, many perceptive critics recoiled in horror when they first discovered its presence in the wartime novel. The unfavorable reaction to the book would undoubtedly have been stronger had it not been recognized as so palpably a propaganda piece, an impassioned defense of democracy against totalitarian terror. The guerrilla figures of *All Night Long* and the struggle they conduct against the Nazis look back to eighteenth-century traditions of sensibility and the natural goodness of man, and to Walter Scott's demonstration that fictional characters could be enhanced by the framework of an actual historical event. These ideas had been long popularized in America, of course, by Fenimore Cooper and his imitators and were enshrined by Hollywood which, not surprisingly, lost no time in purchasing movie rights to the book.

After *All Night Long,* Caldwell published *Georgia Boy* (1943), reshaping earlier short materials into a novel that is really several independent short stories linked together. W. M. Frohock called it with some accuracy years ago "a sort of *Tobacco Road* sweetened down for the carriage trade," and "something like what Mark Twain might have done had he come from Georgia and found himself in a playful mood, and if he wanted to be sure of not offending his public."² It may be true that Caldwell did exercise uncharacteristic reticence in this novel, but for the most part he cared much less than Mark Twain about "offending his public." Rather, in turning to the adolescent point of view he had sometimes used in the short stories, he found it neither necessary nor appropriate to treat sexual matters with his usual explicitness. Because of its point of view, however, fuller discussion of *Georgia Boy* is reserved for the next chapter.

Tragic Ground

Tragic Ground, the last novel published in the crowded years between 1936 and 1944, is in superficial respects protypically Caldwell, much more so than the earlier *Trouble in July,* but its publication marks an end to the era of his critical recognition—though not yet to his status as a minor American celebrity. The book shows a marked similarity in theme and characterization to his novels of the early thirties (grotesques coping with the old problems of unemployment, bad housing, and too little food) and a kinship with later ones in setting, though it is not nearly so rich as *Tobacco Road* or *God's Little Acre.* To create Spence Douthit, his grotesque protagonist, Caldwell turned back to Jeeter Lester for inspiration. In this respect, *Tragic Ground* provides a *goetterdaemmerung* for his most renowned characterization, the unshaven, oversexed rustic, whose casual cruelty and apathetic noncomprehension of the world about him touched the

American funnybone while it seared its conscience. Moreover, both books manage to portray the South in transition, a fact that helps refute the frequent claim that Caldwell remained permanently moored in the South of the New Deal.

Trouble in July

In contrast to Spence, the bumbling Sheriff Jeff McCurtain of *Trouble in July* displays a perception denied the patriarchs of the early novels. Obviously derived from the bulky candidate for sheriff of *God's Little Acre*, Pluto Swint, Jeff McCurtain is a very different man from his literary ancestor. Though McCurtain would be the first to deny himself in any fashion a "nigger lover," he shows an uncharacteristic concern toward Sam Brinson, a "Geechee nigger." When Sam Brinson is abducted from jail by a band of white men searching for Sonny Clark, McCurtain feels an obligation to find him before he is harmed, insisting at one point to his apathetic deputies that "Sam Brinson is a sort of special friend of mine, even if he is a colored man. I just couldn't stand having something bad happen to him." But his concern for the black man does not extend to a willingness to interfere with the lynching of Sonny Clark, for such interference might endanger his election possibilities. *Trouble in July* is so overwhelmingly concerned with the theme of racial justice that proletarian issues scarcely surface in the book except when Caldwell makes the ironic point that the black's most bitter persecutor is the man who has most in common with him, the victimized sharecropper or tenant farmer.

Tragic Ground, the Story of Life in an Urban Subculture

Because *Tragic Ground* is so persistently reminiscent of the kind of longer fiction Caldwell wrote from 1931 to the end of the decade, it is fitting to consider it before its chronological predecessor, *Trouble in July*. In addition, the former presents a more vividly explicit example of Caldwell's belief in the necessary formulation of character through environment. The impact of environment, that of a wartime shantytown in *Tragic Ground* or a redneck Georgia county in *Trouble in July*, is the great shaping influence in the lives of the protagonists of these two novels.

Unlike Jeeter Lester or Ty Ty Walden, Spence Douthit is rarely moved from within. He is neither divinely possessed, nor an instinctual natural man, however much he might resemble Jeeter and Ty Ty in other, less important ways. He is, moreover, Caldwell's embodiment of the effects of life in a subculture, in this book graphically represented by Poor Boy, a shanty town of a Gulfport city that more affluent citizens itch to eradicate. For the first time Caldwell literally—rather than just figuratively—isolates a character from the world about him by banishing him to a recognizable ghetto. This ostracism subserves the central thesis of the novel that character is determined by surrounding, and Caldwell is as insistently naturalistic on this point—in a novel that boasts its share of girls of the street—as Crane was in *Maggie*. It is the author of *Tragic Ground,* not just his character, who is thinking aloud when Spence mulls over a neighbor's murder of his daughter's seducer: "He could not see any sense in trying to maintain beliefs to live by when he had no control over his existence, for no matter how strongly he struggled against his fate, he was never able to master it. At the same time, however, he could not keep from admiring Floyd's attempt to change the course of his existence; but regardless of Floyd's success or failure, Spence still believed that life in Poor Boy was as easy to predict as the rising and setting of the sun, and that even murder could do little to change it."

Spence Douthit, whose story *Tragic Ground* relates, is a tired man of "almost fifty" who has been out of work nearly a year since the gunpowder plant closed. Spence has no idea why his job disappeared nor do we since the war is still raging. But the pedestrian facts of the war and the economy concern Caldwell no more here than did the details of the mill strike in *God's Little Acre*. Spence's wife, Maud, is apparently dying. Bedridden, suffering intermittent bouts of chills and fevers, she lies all day on a cot, clad in a nightgown that constantly slips off her emaciated frame, hoping that Spence will return home carrying a bottle of "Dr. Munday," the alcoholic stomach tonic she feels relieves her suffering.

We meet Spence, another of Caldwell's protagonist victims, at a low ebb in his life, though he is still able to stave off total disaster. A living rebuttal of Aristotle's definition of man as a "rational animal," Spence is instead as irrational, indecisive, and lazy a creature as Caldwell ever drew. Having spent the day fruitlessly searching for a bottle of Dr. Munday on credit, he returns rejectedly to the house only to discover his daughter Libby in bed with Jim Howard Vance, a recuperating soldier originally from the Douthits' old home, Queaseley County, Georgia. This situation, lovers abed observed by a third party, is a device Caldwell had used often before. Spence reacts to the stimulus in a predictably unpredictable fashion. Like other characters of Caldwell's fiction, his curiosity surpasses any other emotional response. After a token show of disapproval, he engages Jim Howard in conversation, an effort that indicates to the reader how totally excluded this looker-on is from a vital life of his own.

When he learns the two plan to marry, he can only measure their decision in selfish terms. On the one hand, he experiences something like paternal pride that "the one member of the family who had always respected the conventions of life" would return legally married to Georgia. On the other hand, he is deeply concerned that he may now be cut off from his only source of income, the little gifts of money he receives from Libby's largesse. Moreover he is reminded that his younger daughter Mavis, only thirteen, has not been home for three or four nights. While Spence considers casually where she might be and how he and Maud can continue to survive in Poor Boy without Libby's assistance, Mrs. Jouett appears at the door to relieve the lull Caldwell uneasily senses.

Satire in *Tragic Ground*

The introduction of Mrs. Jouett and her assistant Miss Saunders, a municipal social worker, gives Caldwell the dual opportunity in a series of anecdotes to indulge in light social satire of do-good philanthropy, a comedic form absent in his other books, and to provide a norm against which the grotesque figures of the subculture may be measured. Miss Saunders, a literal and unimaginative novice totally unprepared for the challenge the Douthits offer, serves the Douthits as a foil. Approaching them with maximum goodwill, she finds herself constantly rebuffed and betrayed. Because neither has insight into how the other thinks, both are constantly misled. Maud, a vigorous harridan despite her illness, concludes the pretty visitor is a "necktie seller," a sort of itinerant prostitute Caldwell had made use of in *Georgia Boy* the year before, and is determined to keep the young woman away from Spence, threatening at one point to "slap those fluffy tits . . . to hell and gone."

The behavior of the Douthits is outrageous, or as Joseph Warren Beach observes about Caldwell's grotesques,

At every turn they violate our notions of decency and good sense. They are like animals of some inferior species, or like little children not yet trained in the ways of adults. But they are dressed and labeled men; they have stature and responsibilities of adults. If we judged them strictly as men, we should have no choice but to be severe. But what prevents us from judging them so is their utter helplessness and ignorance, their incredible innocence, their total lack of awareness that their behavior is shocking.[3]

Unlike the clearly conventional satire leveled at the social workers, the depiction of the Douthits depends on Caldwell's own raucous black humor, in pristine form for the last time. But there is method to this depiction of what first appears merely outlandish. When Spence takes advantage of Miss Saunders, spending for drinking, gambling, Dr. Munday, and flashy clothes the money she has advanced him for rent, water, and bus fare to Beaseley County, he demonstrates symbolically the inability of the subculture to adjust to new circumstances. Spence can only behave erratically when new wealth replaces old poverty. In short, both Spence's wild spree and Maud's paranoia are meant to show the effects caused in one by a radical change in environment. Thus, although he writes of Georgia poor whites in the forties trying to adjust to life in a Hooverville of the Gulf, Caldwell could just as well have used the same methods to describe the difficulties Kentucky hillbillies faced, displaced to Detroit in the mid and late sixties, in acclimating to that vastly different way of life. The best comic scenes of the novel always depend upon just this sort of symbolic representation.

Spence Douthit as Confidence Man

But if Spence is another naif, he is oddly enough a small-scale confidence man too. In this role, however, he bears little resemblance to Semon Dye who made his living selling religion to credulous poor whites. Semon Dye was generally two steps ahead of his victims, whereas Spence is often two behind them. He is a combination of the placid "little man" of the thirties popularized by Hans Fallada's best seller, perhaps even of the "schlemiel" of Jewish sources, but also a "trickster." He is a degenerate Hermes or, more accurately, a Southern Till Eulenspiegel, who enlists low wit and cunning in a ceaseless struggle with opponents of superior means. Not in the least innovative, Spence never originates schemes like Semon Dye; rather he

reacts or responds to some indignity he has suffered or to some wayward opportunity that has come his way. Although he often broods
about injustices or plots revenge against those who have offended
him, he is not obsessed with such thoughts. In fact, he often forgets
them and sometimes has to make a mental note to pursue some devious plan at a convenient future time, as when he reminds himself
to attempt the seduction of Chet Mitchell's wife in order to revenge
himself on the neighbor who led Mavis astray.

When Spence learns from welfare authorities that the police have
located Mavis working at a disreputable roadhouse, the White Tur-
key, he first accepts the news with the fatalistic resignation we have
learned to expect from Caldwell's characters. "Dogbite it," he exclaims hopelessly in such situations, "dogbite my pecker." But it is
at exactly such moments that the trickster surfaces. An enterprising
man need not feel after all "like a rabbit with his balls caught in a
sewing machine." For example, to save Mavis from her own lascivious
appetites, Spence conceives the plan of marrying her to the first eli-
gible male he can find, a scheme exuding the same black humor we
have just seen, since the act of marrying off Mavis involves a grotesque imitation of conventional behavior based on a pathetic trust
that the institution of matrimony can avert the chaos promiscuity so
often entails.

The petty deceits practiced against.the Welfare Department or the
tricks Spence plays on others offer no revolutionary threat to the social order, no rule of fools. He is only a gadfly, driven to such ruses
by outside forces: poverty, ignorance, desire for revenge or hunger,
and an interior lack of direction. His behavior is largely "automatic
and inevitable, the outcome of economic pressure and conforming to
a primitive code."[4] Spence can fight back with great cunning, but he
is inspired in life by no ruling passion as were Jeeter Lester, Will
Thompson, and Semon Dye. He suffers a deficiency of heroism. He
never seeks to challenge his destiny, only to compromise with it. Yet
the forces that victimize him are not altogether relentless. His straits
are not quite desperate. Perhaps he is too irresponsible to be affected
by the world. Because nothing is sacred to him (not even Mavis and
Maud, whom he considers abandoning since Mavis, he reasons, can
support herself and her mother with her gains from the White Tur-
key), he has arrived without seeking it at the enviable state longed
for by stoic philosophers. When we last see Spence, headed home to

Beaseley County on the bus as commanded by welfare authorities, he is slyly confiding to Maud his scheme to return to Poor Boy as soon as he can borrow the fare from Jim Howard Vance. Till Eulenspiegel has escaped his hanging.

Contrasts with Earlier Novels

Tragic Ground reintroduces a variety of subjects familiar from Caldwell's earlier work, but it also ignores many of the themes that had previously attracted him. The humor is still present, as is a certain amount of violence, the serious use of grotesquerie, and a barely repressed mistrust of women. But *Tragic Ground* does not contain a single black character,[5] and the important primitivist, Dionysian, and proletarian themes are gone or altered beyond recognition. The only vestige, for example, of the celebration of male sexuality that so suffused *God's Little Acre* is a scant notice that Jim Howard Vance displays an admirable vitality and confidence in taking Libby to mate. In his last appearance, he is seen confidently guiding the bewildered family to the bus, a protective arm tightly around Libby while he refutes Mrs. Jouett's charge that people like the Douthits are incorrigible by nature with a proletarian rebuttal: "It's not our fault that everything got into a mess down here. Back home people like us are just as good as people anywhere else in the world. If you want to do the right thing, you ought to put all the blame on Poor Boy, because it's Poor Boy that causes all the trouble. The finest folks in the world would get mean and bad if they had to live in a place like this. That's why you ought to run Poor Boy out of town instead of running people out."

Environment as a Behavioral Determinant in *Tragic Ground*

It is this environmentalist theme with its necessary ramifications that forms the central thesis of *Tragic Ground.* More in the vein of a Benjamin Franklin than as a radical of the Roosevelt era to be excoriated by *Red Channels,* Caldwell argues throughout his novel that depressed surroundings produce scarred people, that vice and crime can be extirpated only if the surroundings that breed them are abolished.

Mavis, her friend Florabelle, and Justine, daughter of Spence's only friend, Floyd Sharp, all corrupted by the poverty and boredom of shantytown life, serve as the chief examples of the sexual degradation that Poor Boy spawns. Caldwell makes some effort to accuse capitalism for the existence of the slum, and in an aside furnished by Jim Howard Vance, he attacks slum landlords briefly as he attacked rural landlords briefly in *Tobacco Road*: "The ones who own this land are to blame for not putting up better houses, and the city is to blame for not doing something about it. You know yourself it's nothing but a rat hole, and people can't live like human beings very long in a rat hole." But Caldwell allows Jim Howard to proceed a step or two farther in righteous indignation: "If places like this don't get wiped off the map, I'll be sort of sorry I ever went to war and had my eyes opened. You feel like all the shooting and fighting on the other side of the world didn't amount to much when you come back and find Poor Boys scattered all around the country."

Though Jim Howard's argument is not strictly coherent, it strikes a familiar chord. Its tone is prewar and has a Depression-era ring. We must remember that Caldwell wrote this speech before America saw victory in Europe. Jim Howard plays the familiar role of the disillusioned veteran, as he had been already seen by Dos Passos or Odets. His socialist wrath is the same shared, for example, by Moe Axelrod in *Awake and Sing!* some nine years earlier. In fact, Caldwell himself must have felt the scorn of the returned soldier when he saw how little the war he had championed in books and articles, in bond drives and broadcasts from "the other side of the world," was doing to eliminate social injustice.

The situation of the Douthits is reminiscent, too, of the displaced Oakies of *The Grapes of Wrath*. Like the Joads, the Douthits are victims of economic and environmental forces beyond their understanding. But if *Tragic Ground* falls well below the accomplishment of *The Grapes of Wrath*, Caldwell must at least be credited for taking a more balanced view of his protagonists than did Steinbeck. With his ever fluctuating opinion of the worth of the common man and his wavering trust in self-reliance, Caldwell spared no pains to depict the unpleasant side of Spence Douthit. Lacking even Jeeter's saving grace, a genuine love for the soil, Spence's lamentable state is to a considerable extent self-induced. We are touched to learn "It had been almost three years since he had talked to anyone from home, and there were several times when his homesickness was so intense that he did not believe he could keep on living any longer." But that is only one side of the story, as becomes apparent shortly. Spence is loath to leave Poor Boy for a variety of reasons. Most important is the inertia that guides men's affairs. "Bodies at rest tend to remain at rest"—that is the great principle dominating the behavior of Caldwell's early protagonists. In addition to a natural inertia, Spence has become accustomed to the dole granted him by Libby, and he does not gladly anticipate the labor required to earn a living back home in Georgia. Libby, a sensible young woman who knows her mind and who marks a change from the subservient females Caldwell so often drew before *Journeyman,* advises her father to leave immediately, but suspects with good reason that he wishes to stay: "There's no excuse for staying here any longer," she says. "You can find Mavis if you'll go out and look for her, and you can sell the furniture for enough money for the bus fare home. I can't give you and Ma any more money after I stop working in town and go away with Jim Howard. You'll have to do something yourself from then on." But Spence argues that return is impossible for "everybody knows I can't find me a job, Libby. . . . I just ain't got the strength in my body to tussle with a thing like that no more." Libby then prods a sensitive spot: ". . . you know life's a lot easier down here. If you went back up there, you'd have to farm in summer and cut wood in winter. Down here you don't have to do a blessed thing as long as somebody comes around every week and hands you a few dollars."

If Libby's accusation is just, as Spence later tacitly acknowledges it is, Caldwell's social-protest argument appears to lose some of its force. But in this message as elsewhere, he refused to commit himself unreservedly to one view. That the squalor and disorder of Poor Boy contribute to broken lives is evident from numerous sorry examples the story provides; on the other hand, Spence himself is relatively happy living there, so happy that at the moment he must leave the shantytown his eyes fill with tears, and he unobtrusively gathers up a "handful of smooth round pebbles" from in front of his house because he "had to have something that he could touch and look at as a rememberance of Poor Boy." Caldwell, in short, skirts the issue. Perhaps it is his degrading poverty more than his surroundings that dispirits Spence, for when he earned $62.50 a week the Douthits suffered no insurmountable difficulties. In those days, an excitement and vitality existed in the slovenly, crowded neighborhood of new arrivals.

Value of Labor

Here Caldwell evokes a subject that had held his interest for many years, the value of labor. Like Faulkner or Ellen Glasgow, Caldwell seems convinced that the apathy and degeneracy that stalk the South are partly attributable to a failure to accord work the respect it deserves. In personal interviews, he seldom failed to stress the unflagging effort demanded of a writer, just as in speaking of his admired father, he invariably recalled the minister at work, whether making pastoral calls to rural families or traveling to remote corners of the South to settle the quarrels of irascible congregations. A work-intoxicated writer who even today cannot depart from a writing schedule, Caldwell realized, too, that the legacy of slavery continued to sap the South of its vitality into modern times. Jeeter Lester, Spence Douthit, and Jeff McCurtain serve as vivid contrasts to Ellen Glasgow's vigorous heroine, Dorinda Oakley, who turns back the broomsedge of her father's Virginia farm, conquering the very environment by the strength of her will. What Walter Allen identified as the major concerns of *Barren Ground* are applicable to much of Caldwell's work: ". . . farmland . . . falling out of cultivation because of the aftermath of the Civil War and the Reconstruction, the breakdown of the traditional social system, the poverty and ignorance of the people and also . . . the engrained Southern habit of 'slighting' work."[6]

Of course, neither Spence Douthit nor Jeff McCurtain earns his living from the soil, though both once did. Jeff is now locked into a soul-destroying office he hates but dares not relinquish, while Spence idles away his days without a job. Meaningful work, however, Caldwell reiterates, is necessary to a man's life, but not the kind of work Spence did at the powder factory, where "every fifteen minutes a bell went clang-clang-clang and a red light flashed on," where he "jumped up and blew a whistle and took a dipperful of the stuff and poured it in a bottle," only to sit patiently for another quarter hour "to do it all over again." Spence might as well have worked at the Lordstown Assembly Plant of General Motors three decades later. Thus, though he remembers his erstwhile prosperity nostalgically, he wishes that he had enjoyed more dignified employment, "a trade like carpentering or barbering or the like." But productive work, Caldwell insists, gives order to life. Spence's tedious job could never truly liberate him as mill work could Will or planting cotton, Jeeter. Yet it was necessary for him. In sin and ignorance, in his basic fallibility, man must toil or he will succumb to a worse fate than that which he presently suffers. In Caldwell's view, God's words to Adam at his expulsion from paradise in Genesis 3:9—"In the sweat of thy face shalt thou eat bread"—are perhaps not so much a curse as a prescription for a tolerable life in a fallen state.

Sexual Themes

The most vulnerable victims of life in Poor Boy are its young girls like Justine, Mavis, and her friend, Florabelle, all children sexually exploited by adults. Yet even here Caldwell stops short of absolute exculpation. Much of the fault for their ruin, he says, lies with their offensive female biology. While he does not mock them outright as he did Ellie May, he still shows impatience with female sexuality a dozen years after *Tobacco Road*. Mavis openly delights in her ability to excite men, and the sexually precocious Justine follows Spence about with such blatantly promiscuous glances that at one point he throws a rock to drive her away. Despite efforts to temper his contempt with the sentimental tale of Florabelle, the abandoned child, the concept of woman as "flowing bitch" still obsesses Caldwell in this novel, where sexual activity is so frequently a sign of degeneracy.

The joyless couplings of *Tragic Ground* serve to demonstrate how limited and fragile a thing is human love, the single quality that lifts man above the beasts. When Bubber, Spence's outlandish choice of a husband for Mavis, escapes him by leaping naked from an open window and is found dallying with Justine in a shed near her house, Floyd loses no time in killing him with an axe blow to the head. This act, motivated by benighted parental concern, is witnessed by Spence, who loyally defends his friend: "Floyd's not the kind to kill nobody unless he had a mighty good reason." But reason-defying logic notwithstanding, Spence knows as well as Clay Horey did, "there ain't no way in heaven or hell of stopping what's bound to be."

Caldwell provides a graphic incident later in the book to demonstrate the inevitability of biological determinism even more forcefully. When Spence and Maud are almost ready to leave for Georgia, the house they have been renting is suddenly occupied by the Clairbornes with their numerous brood. Spence sees no reason to move out early on that account, and in a fashion comprehensible only to those who have read a good number of Caldwell's bed-swapping scenes, he finds himself "snuggled up against" Jessica, the fifteen-year-old daughter of these impoverished people who have come to try their luck in Poor Boy. Spence is on the verge of making love to her when an interruption occurs. Thus it is only by fortuitous circumstance that he is kept from inflicting on Jessica the sexual initiation that Chet Mitchell gave Mavis and Bubber gave Justine.

Conclusion

Spence's moral myopia and his total irrationality are our own greatly magnified, but that of Caldwell's previous protagonists somewhat shrunken. Spence certainly qualifies as a grotesque, but he represents an attempt on his author's part to come closer to the realism he sought with ill success in *A House in the Uplands* (1946), *Place Called Estherville* (1949), and *Love and Money* (1954). The magnification that Zola and Norris practiced was also necessary to Caldwell. Like theirs, his best characters strain heroically at the limitations of realism. But in his lack of depth Spence fails Caldwell. He is only a trickster managing to get along, not an obsessed hero consumed by unanswered longings.

Insofar as he develops or learns about himself, he lags far behind Jeff McCurtain, the protagonist of *Trouble in July*. When Spence thinks of anything, it is half heartedly of his return to Beaseley County. Jeff, on the other hand, has begun to question his place in life and recently to think about the black as well. None of this is to say that he has acquired any profound insight. By conventional standards his remains a benighted mind throughout the novel. In fact, his questionings may never end in realization at all. The conclusion of *Trouble in July,* like so many of the short stories, offers the reader, rather than the protagonist, the opportunity to change. In other words, the epiphany is more the reader's than the character's.[7]

Trouble in July: Plot

Jeff is a bulky, lazy, sweating southern sheriff who constantly worries as he drives the backroads that at the next election he may be voted out of his job and the apartment over the jail that goes with it. Because he is determined to hold this empty job at any cost, he is obliged to close his eyes to the organization of a lynch mob near Flowery Branch, a jurisdiction in Julie County. He does not approve of lynching, but he regards it tolerantly as a weakness of others, almost as an enthusiastic skiier might regard snowmobiling or a bridge player, poker. The psychology of lynching is not Caldwell's chief interest in this story. He had treated it splendidly in the previous decade in "Saturday Afternoon" and "Kneel to the Rising Sun," as Faulkner and Wolfe had treated it in novels and stories as well. In *Trouble in July,* the lynching takes on festive airs, like a coon hunt. A carnival thrill of excitement surrounds the meeting at night, the gatherings in the light of automobile headlamps, the wait for the best dogs to arrive, and the delicious swapping of stories. A lynching is an event to look forward to, a break in the dreary routine of field labor, a chance to avenge oneself on the competitor who works cheaper and harder than oneself, and, most peculiarly of all, an opportunity to assuage one's guilt toward the black by calling attention to his bestial nature and punishing it publicly.

The attitude of Caldwell's poor whites toward a black, a woman, or an albino is extraordinarily callous, measured in civilized terms; but it reminds us of that taken by many a seventeenth-century colonist toward the Indian. Neither believes that the people he deals with are even human. In Caldwell, a southern white man will take a black girl as unequivocally as John Smith or William Bradford seized Indian corn. Joseph Warren Beach writes: "If they do not worry about grandma or the nigger killed by the car, it is because they have never properly taken in the existence of other beings as real as themselves. In Caldwell's short stories the most cold-blooded cruelty is exercised against niggers or women by men who have never learned that women or niggers have serious claims on white men."[8]

Sexual Exploitation and Racism

Sexual exploitation of the black in this book represents what the sexual conquest has meant in other novels, whether it was adults exploiting children or men exploiting women. The sex act, when it is not Dionysian, is an act of hate. Sexual exploitation becomes a metaphor for the absence of charity and the cruelty of racism. But even Jeff has been guilty in the past of demanding sexual favors from the black women in his jail, nor have his deputies abandoned the practice, though he lectures them ceaselessly on the subject: ". . . I don't want to find that cage-room back there full of nigger wenches, either, when I come back. The last time I went off for a few days, I came

back here and found a nigger gal in almost every cage in the whole
jailhouse. . . . I ain't going to stand having this jail turned into a
whorehouse."

Though Jeff has not yet grasped the "serious claims" of the black
nor even totally recognized the black's humanity, he is no mindless,
redneck "nigger-hater." In fact, his deep affection for his tiny wife
offers evidence of the familial attachment Caldwell always attributes
to the good man. But his moral sense is by no means fully developed.
As yet, black-baiting offends his sense of decorum more than his
sense of justice. At the story's present moment, he wishes only to
keep the lynching "politically clean" by being absent on a fishing trip
when the mob finds Sonny Clark. Later he might evolve to a state of
moral outrage. If he hates anyone, it is Narcissa Calhoun, the prototype of all right-wing, meddling, "little old ladies in tennis shoes,"
who is currently circulating a petition to have blacks returned to Af-
rica. Jeff despises her, not just because she causes him additional labor by the bad feeling she generates throughout the county or because
she has coached Katy Barlow into accusing Sonny Clark, but because
she is a bigoted lunatic.

He knows that if Narcissa Calhoun can attract enough attention to
her cause—and herself, since her name is another example of Caldwell's fondness for tags—he, too, will have to add his signature be-
latedly to her petition. Then he will be in bondage to her as he is
presently to Judge Ben Allen, leader of the Allen-Democrats and political county boss. He is dimly aware that "nigger trouble" has the
effect of reducing him to a "nigger" himself, a persecuted "frazzle-
assed" figure afraid to offend the Judge, Narcissa, the mob, or
wealthy landowners like Bob Watson, who understands that Sonny
Clark's lynching will send every black field hand he has into hiding
at "laying-by time."

This ironic reversal of roles whereby the white man learns the black
man's sorrows by figuratively becoming a black man is made especially clear at the end of the novel, when Harvey Glenn turns Sonny
Clark over to the mob out of fear that he himself will be taken for a
"nigger-lover." Aware from Sonny's story that the boy is innocent of
any wrongdoing, Harvey Glenn explains awkwardly that he is bound
by local mores to violate his conscience: ". . . this is white-man's
country. Niggers has always had to put up with it. . . . It's just the
way things is, I reckon." Even more ironical, however, is the fact
that Harvey Glenn's words are almost a paraphrase of the Latin ob-

servation of the aristocratic, and possibly perverted, Judge Allen to an uncomprehending Jeff: "Consuetudo manerii [*sic*] et loci est observanda."

Of course, undeviating adherence to local customs can only benefit petty tyrants like the Judge. And Caldwell suggests in this novel that he and others are committed to maintain an environment meant to mold the characters of those around them to their own advantage. Jeff, like almost everyone else in Julie County—black or white—is enslaved by degrading customs and manipulated by the unscrupulous persons who profit from their obedience to an outmoded code. Consequently, Jeff's vision of racial justice is indeed dim, even cynical, but the important thing is that he has one at all; and that represents an enormous evolution from Jeeter's fatalistic conclusion that "niggers will get killed," an attitude subscribed to by Ty Ty Walden, Clay Horey, and Semon Dye as well. Jeff understands, as they did not, that there is no reason for the black man to suffer at the white man's hand; and though he lacks the courage to do much about it in the face of organized opposition, his recognition may suggest eventual change, Caldwell's long view of history. The Old Testament–like stoning of Kathy by the mob when she confesses her lie and the mutilated body of Sonny hanging at the end of a rope change Jeff permanently. Appalled, he mutters, "It ought to put an end to lynching the colored for all time."

Caldwell has not really explained how Jeff reaches the modicum of tolerant enlightenment he now achieves, except to imply that the charity he has gruffly practiced with Sam Brinson, the "Geechee nigger," has saved him. In fact, Caldwell never states categorically that such a change occurs at all. Jeff's next remark, indeed, is an asinine comment about his duty to report the crime; but his previous display of horror, the avoidance of his usual epithet "nigger," and his symbolic gesture of silently stepping out ahead of the others, alone, to return to his car—all these are encouraging signs. Caldwell seems to be saying that charity—here, love of one's fellow man—can someday triumph over the outrage of racial injustice.

Chapter Six
The Role of the Short Stories

From the late twenties until about 1959, when he virtually abandoned the short story to concentrate on the novel, Caldwell published about 150 short stories. These run broadly parallel to the novels in theme and style, declining in quality as they do, and finally disappearing at the end of the same decade in which the death knell sounded for his popular reputation. But the importance of this body of stories cannot be exaggerated, for as we have periodically seen, they were the great trying ground for the novels. Here in the short stories, Caldwell developed the themes of his novels and molded his prose style. But because his novels remain episodic and anecdotal throughout his career, the stories may well have had a debilitating effect on his longer fiction. Too often, for example, he contrives an epiphany in a novel where none is structurally justified. The sudden end to an incident, so effective in the brief story, sometimes gives evidence in a longer work only of a failure to achieve a satisfactory closure. For almost fifty years, Caldwell's fiction was dominated by a short story habit.[1]

On the positive side, however, the genre represented his first efforts to be published and always remained his great love and proudest achievement. In his mind, the quickly told story and fiction remain synonymous. Almost everything he says about writing in *Call It Experience* and many of his critical pronouncements are more easily understood when this fact is realized. His competitive sense, an inward prompting that bordered on a sense of threat and proceeded from a deep insecurity,[2] drove him to the novel long before he was ready. Maxwell Perkins's advice, large royalties, and the enormous popularity of *Tobacco Road* and *God's Little Acre* conspired to hold him to that route. But like his contemporaries Hemingway, Fitzgerald, and Faulkner, writers with whom he was once perceived to be in competition, Caldwell came of age nourished by a conviction that the short story was the true measure of the creative writer's worth.

The figure of 150 stories is only approximate and does not indicate how many others were written and discarded or filed away and forgotten. Caldwell often held stories for many years before including them in collections, and he frequently introduced them in new or disguised forms. Thus, to choose some arbitrary examples, "The Story of Mahlon," published in *When You Think of Me* (1959), Caldwell's last collection, appears to have been written very early, judging by its melancholy impressionistic style. This was a style he rejected after the *Sacrilege of Alan Kent* (1929–31), although he returned to it periodically, as certain passages in novels like *Gretta* (1955) testify. On the other hand, "A Visit to Mingus County" from the same collection appears to date from the robust years when he still saw the rural South as a land of great comic potential, and when he regularly wrote short stories about the glories or troubles inflicted by one's kinfolk, stories like "The Windfall" (1942) or "Uncle Ned's Short Stay" (1943). Moreover, "Uncle Ned's Short Stay" was later incorporated as a chapter in the novel *Georgia Boy*, just as, in a somewhat contrary fashion, he extracted prose sections like "Bread in Uzok" and "Wine of Surany" from the prewar *North of the Danube*, written with Margaret Bourke-White, and called them "stories" for inclusion in *When You Think of Me*.

The short stories, then, offer us a kind of microcosm of Caldwell's artistic achievement and of his success. The early ones tend to appear in little magazines or national publications such as *Scribner's*, the *New Yorker*, *Collier's*, *transition*, *Story*, and the *Yale Review*, whereas the later ones find doubtful refuge in pulps like *Dude*, *Cavalier*, *Swank*, and *Manhunt* or in obscure European periodicals. This does not mean that every early story is genuinely meritorious, however. On the contrary, the stories serve as more sensitive barometers of his ability than the novels. Less memorable pieces abound from the start. In fact, the weaknesses that plague Caldwell after *God's Little Acre* surface in many of the earliest stories. The bathos absent from *Tobacco Road* and *God's Little Acre*, the awkward dialogue and pompousness not apparent in these novels, occur periodically in many early stories. In these years, Caldwell's consuming interest in female psychology found expression delicately in *Tobacco Road*, exuberantly in *God's Little Acre*, and sometimes clumsily as in "Dorothy" (1931) or "Carnival" (1936).

Women in the Stories

His writing—despite the often contrary impression—is of a single piece. He maintains a consistent interest in situations and states of mind, even when he abandons one social class for another or adjusts to new problems facing a later generation. So it is with his lifelong concern with the role of women, especially his barely repressed fear of their domination. Sometimes he is able to suggest, sensitively but with humor, his mistrust of women as in *Georgia Boy*—a novel that began as the short story "My Old Man." Here he borrows from Hemingway not only the title but the attitude that Hemingway and Anderson so often expressed—that the company of men is a finer thing than that of women. Caldwell's approach in that novel is humorous and understated. It manifests itself mostly through a careful point of view, that of a young boy, subject to maternal authority but clearly more sympathetic to the men around him.

As early as 1929, however, he had terrifyingly objectified his concept of smothering womanhood in a menacing female figure tagged blatantly Mrs. Boxx. An illegal abortionist and hater of youth, this repulsive woman has somehow had her husband castrated (an ineffectual necrophiliac!) and seeks to inflict the same punishment on Blondy Niles, the young boxer-protagonist of this disturbed novel. More than four decades after *Poor Fool*, Mrs. Boxx's attitude finds expression again in *The Earnshaw Neighborhood* (1971), less offensively to be sure, but articulated in terms recognizably borrowed from the eerie expressionistic novel written in his twenties.

The mannish Medora Earnshaw, like Mrs. Boxx a woman exhibiting strong sexual desires for young men, renders her mild second husband, Beejay Leffaway, impotent through the intense psychic pressures she exerts on him. As in the early novel, the older woman encourages a nubile daughter to lure virile young men to their house. Her husband displays signs of voyeurism like his predecessor in *Poor Fool* (and dozens of other novels and stories), and at one point achieves considerable sexual titillation, not with a corpse, but by spanking a mannequin. For all its weaknesses, *The Earnshaw Neighborhood* cannot simply be dismissed as a work of his dotage, however, because it is packed with so many of the ingredients Caldwell manipulated over and over again in his prime. For example, in this novel that is half-soap opera, half-farce, Caldwell provides a pandemonic scene reminiscent of the kind he had delighted in since "Country Full of Swedes" won him a Yale Review Award for Fiction in the mid-thirties. A tourist bus stops in front of Medora Earnshaw's house, and while she holds the gawking shutterbugs at bay with a garden hose, children, bicycles, dogs, and police cars appear in noisy confusion. The chaos of everyone talking and no one listening or understanding is a variation on the deathly silence of *Tobacco Road,* Caldwell's metaphor for the lack of communication that typifies the human condition.

Humor and the Lack of It

Because his humorous stories are often his best and because he found that a mixture of comedy and pathos characterized his most successful efforts, Caldwell was reluctant to abandon humor altogether. On the other hand, by the closing days of World War II, he was growing weary of the funny man's burden, just as Mark Twain once had. Now he turned in the direction of the literal sort of realism he had rejected many years before to produce short stories about sexual tensions and marriage. Such are the largely humorless and ephemeral stories that fill collections like *Gulf Coast Stories* (1956) and *Certain Women* (1957). Caldwell's decision to de-emphasize humor, if it were a conscious one, seems then to have arisen in the later forties. But even then he is not consistent. *A House in the Uplands* (1946) may be solemn, but *The Sure Hand of God* (1947) has riotous and bawdy moments, and so it goes well into the fifties and sixties. The collection *Gulf Coast Stories* (1956) inspired several novels in the fifties, though contrary to the usual fashion, a novel of this period may have engendered a short story. *Episode in Palmetto* (1950) shows great similarity to "In Memory of Judith Cortright" (1953), and *Gretta* (1950) appears to be an expanded version of "Her Name Was Amelie" (1955). Both of these novels, like *Gulf Coast Stories,* are purged of the old Caldwell humor. *Jenny by Nature* (1961), in contrast to these earlier books, is often humorous, though it too appears to have been inspired by a story from the *Gulf Coast* collection, the bittersweet tale, "The Shooting of Judge Price," that first appeared in 1956 in *Playboy.*

Later Stories

Perhaps, however, the title piece of his last story collection "When You Think of Me" (1959), a melodramatic tale of a returned veteran's attempt to honor a promise to a dead comrade, may be said to set the pace for his novels of the fifties and sixties. The result is seldom happy. The de-emphasis of humor, the avoidance of backcountry Georgia, and the attempt to write seriously about mature subjects (while occasionally reverting to the literary folktale) did not work, though it indicates that Caldwell was experimenting in the fifties just as he had in the thirties. But experimentation notwithstanding, Margaret Bourke-White's charge made in *Portrait of Myself* (1967) has merit, that Caldwell was writing the same things over again and not as well. She saw him "barricading himself from new experience," and her judgment shows considerable perception.

Caldwell's best early stories had dazzled sophisticated readers for—among other virtues—his casually unimpeachable documentation. In describing a Maine or Georgia setting, he communicated a sense of utter familiarity with his subject. He seemed to have limitless knowledge about such recondite topics as hiring an Indian, breeding leghorns, selling a Kennebec farm, or capturing a runaway jackass. His easy allusions to a host of unfamiliar activities bespeak a confidence that makes Hemingway's similar technique appear at times academic by comparison. He exudes effortless authority of the kind that Crane searched the streets of New York trying to acquire or that sent Dreiser to upstate New York court transcripts.

In the forties, fifties, and sixties, by contrast, this sense is gone. Caldwell, now a resident of Connecticut, Arizona, California, or Florida, begins gradually writing about the middle class, a more complicated breed than Georgia backcountry sharecroppers or Vermont farmers, and one that he failed to capture in words. He describes novelists—*Love and Money* (1954)—now more familiar to him than tenant farmers, but a race as distant to him as college professors, and post-Depression blacks who equally escape him. The problems of writing outside experience, however, were not new to him. They had occurred in *The Bastard, Poor Fool,* and a number of stories like "Dorothy" (1930) and "Martha Jean" (1935), attempts at female psychology and a tough city life that he knew only at several removes. But now they threatened to engulf him, for he made the mistake of providing the language and sentiments appropriate in rural characters to those of loftier status and of mixing grotesques with conventionally realistic figures in his novels. Finally, of course, he dropped the short stories, without doubt partly because publication opportunities had declined, but also because he knew the truth of Washington Irving's acknowledgment: "in shorter writings, every page must have its merit."[3] Thus, the short stories not only run a parallel course with the novels, but in a real sense they draw them along from the late twenties to the early fifties.[4]

Style and Influences

Today Caldwell's critical reputation rests on two novels still selling more than forty years after publication. But neither *Tobacco Road* nor *God's Little Acre* would have been possible without the previous discipline of the short stories. It is not just the Georgia background, the proletarian concern, or the original characters[5] that make them so memorable, it is their style. From the short stories, Caldwell brought to the novels epiphany, the speedy climactic episode, the deceptively languorous anecdote, and the American sentences whose very prosaic bluntness served to frame with appropriate modesty the marvels that lay within the stories themselves.

Because Caldwell tried his hand at so many different kinds of stories, it is difficult to classify them satisfactorily. There are many of adolescent sexual awakening, of Depression enormities, and of what might vaguely be called "lost love." But the best are usually humorous tales with rural settings or accounts of the cruelty and injustice regularly visited upon the black.[6] Some of the latter like "Saturday Afternoon" (1930) depend upon a cruel Southern gallows humor and bitter irony that the literal failed to see in *Tobacco Road;* others like "Kneel to the Rising Sun" (1935) are more conventionally told. "Kneel to the Rising Sun" contains a strong proletarian strain, but it eschews the leftist melodrama of many of Caldwell's Depression pieces by avoiding a city background and by skillfully melding social elements with the plight of the rural black. His stories of sexual awakening and of the buried life of the village show a heavy influence of Sherwood Anderson, for Caldwell was certainly one of the "children of Sherwood Anderson" as Faulkner aptly noted. But the Hemingway influence was perhaps equally strong, though that influence is almost exclusively stylistic, whereas Anderson's is an influence of both style and theme. In "Joe Craddock's Old Woman" (1929), the story of a work-scarred drab who is transformed in death to a bride's beauty, Caldwell writes:

Death was her compensation. As it came it was compensation for the ugliness of her face and body, and of her life. She had been miserable while she lived—eleven children, fourteen cows, and a flock of chickens.—And eight stinking hogs. Not once had Julia left the farm in over ten years. Work, work, work, from four in the morning till nine at night; never a vacation, a trip to town nor time to bathe all over. Joe worked all the time, too. Yet his labor returned nothing but an aching back, heartbreak, and poverty. The harder he worked the poorer he became. If he made twenty bales of cotton in the fall the price would drop to where he could barely pay for the fertilizer—usually not even that. Or if the price went up to thirty cents a pound he would, by the curse of too much rain or not enough rain, have no cotton to sell. There with Joe and Julia life wasn't worth living very long.[7]

The theme of the wasted rural life is quintessentially Andersonian, though admittedly from Garland to Sinclair Lewis and Faulkner it is a staple of American literature. Also in the manner of Anderson are the apparently casual but pertinently unpleasant details ("eleven children"), culminating in an impatient "eight stinking hogs." Typical, too, is the narrative voice that grows faintly distant and pretentiously philosophic at one moment but at the next becomes overeager to assure us of the depth of its sympathy for its humble subjects. It tacitly assures us that it speaks the language of the people described ("work, work, work" and "the price would drop to where he could barely pay"), that it understands their "heartbreak" and modest aspiration while articulating them through the use of words like "compensation" and "labor."

Altogether different and far less derivative is "The Automobile That Wouldn't Run," published the next year. Here Caldwell is more his own man, telling how Mal Anderson, a stolid Swede lumberjack, tricked the boss woodsman. Sent to catch two runaway "Canucks" fleeing the logging camp by canoe, Mal overtakes them easily on the river and then continues to run away himself. Caldwell does not leave the story here, however. Already he had learned that he could often achieve a good effect by taking some stories back to where they had started by letting them down from climactic excitement to a calmer moment. Thus, in the final pages of "The Automobile That Wouldn't Run," Mal Anderson is returned to his original situation, sitting in the back seat of his permanently disabled car, wordlessly plunking a banjo, serenading the proprietress of the Penobscot Hotel. Great moments and wild shenanigans are all very well, Caldwell seems to say. They add spice to life and fiction, but real life, real meaning, is to be found in sitting and waiting.

This story is uniquely his own in mood, tone, and theme, but the prose style betrays the influence that Fitzgerald had sarcastically noted, insisting that it had first passed through the alembic of Morely Callaghan: "Signe ran the Penobscot Hotel. It was a woodsman's hotel. The men used it when they came to town to spend the money they made up in the woods. Signe ran the hotel without help. She did not need any." The flat declarative sentence that Hemingway was making famous appears here in unadorned subject-verb order five times in succession. Even the effect of variety introduced by the subordinate clauses of the third sentence is vitiated by the monotonous primer style of the passage's short concluding two sentences. Fitzgerald's derision may have some substance here. Caldwell was indeed imitating Hemingway at this point, and the echoes keep occurring in this story. A bit later, for example, we are told: "Scott went down the road without looking back once. Scott was a brave boss woodsman."

Nonetheless, during these same years, about 1929 to 1933, Caldwell successfully hammered out the inimitable style and technique that characterize his best and most representative stories. In place of Anderson's solemnity, Caldwell invented a noisy, grotesque way of treating similar subject matter just as meaningfully as his mentor, but more ebulliently. Both writers sought to express the powerful force of sex in motivating men and women in rural settings and to show how the force so often inhibits, rather than enriches life. But Caldwell's stories are not delicate sketches, at once realistic and psychological like Anderson's. Caldwell paints with a palette knife, smearing flamboyant daubs of humor and gross characterization with vivid colors across his small canvas. His work looks primitive beside Anderson's, but it is vivid and pulsating too. In "Meddlesome Jack" (1933), a young wife, frightened and sexually aroused by the braying of a jackass, seizes her husband across the kitchen table and must be literally shaken off: "Daisy fell down on the kitchen floor, holding on to his legs with all her might." The cliché, "all her might," works well here, reducing the dramatic gesture to low comedy. At the end of the tale, the girl heads down the road to run off with a sailor, but her deserted husband has learned that the yearnings unleashed by the "jack's" blatant sexuality can be directed many ways. Or as an old black retainer knowingly advises: "Looks like that jack has a powerful way of fretting the women folks, and you'd better get him to turn one in your direction."

Of course, by no stretch of the imagination can Caldwell be called a stylist, even at the peak of his power in the thirties. Like Dreiser, whom one despairing critic called "the Hindenburg of the novel," he often succeeds despite infelicities of prose. "Language," as Robert Hazel has said of him, "is no particular friend of his and he has to go it alone, the hard way of a writer who has not found within him the capacity to love language."[8]

Caldwell taught himself to write a taut conversational style that in the end betrayed him, for he came finally to believe that whatever can be said can be written, or worse, that whatever comes to mind can be written. He had always been willing to stray, when he believed it necessary, from the purity of the Hemingway-like sentence he sought early in his career. But the result often became prosaic and flat. Inevitably the length of his sentences increased, though they continued to maintain a syntactical simplicity. In no way do Caldwell's longer sentences emulate the grammatical intricacies of a Henry James or the aggressive self-confidence of a Faulkner. Instead, they become merely overweight and ungainly. The year of *Tobacco Road,* 1932, Caldwell started "Over the Green Mountains" with a sprightly declarative sentence, imitating the New England down-east dialect: "Was reading a piece in the Boston paper last night about the smartest people in the whole country coming from the State of Maine." In his last novel, *Annette* (1973), with the discipline of regular short story publication many years behind him, he writes, "During the recent months of Annette's marriage to Dean Thurmond, while living with him in the large and imposing graystone house on a high terrace in the rolling green hills of Zephyrfield, a quiet residential suburb of costly homes and estates several miles from Dean's law offices in the busy industrial city of Melbourne, there were numerous times when Annette was on the verge of leaving home."[9]

Language and Dialogue

The difference is remarkable. Not only is the second sentence pompous and ungainly, it also displays a failure to differentiate between what is important and what is not. His ear for language was never sharp. But at one time he knew it, and he avoided exposing his weakness by taking few chances. He kept his sentences uncomplicated, his diction simple, and avoided contractions. The result is a colloquial dignity, at its finest, representative of authentic American English. Avoiding the rhetorical and the poetical—both of which meant claptrap to the young southerner who had spent a boyhood listening to pulpit oratory—he wrote instead a factual prose, innocent of all but the most pedestrian figures of speech, a prose designed to advance the narration of the story and highlight the dialogue. Often it has a faintly awkward rural tone, as if the speaker were an articulate farmer:

To George Williams went the distinction of being the first to suggest making Sam Billings the new town treasurer. The moment he made the nomination at the annual town meeting there was an enthusiastic chorus of approval that resulted in the first unanimous election in the history of Androscoggin. During the last of the meeting everybody was asking himself why no one had ever thought of Sam Billings before.

Even in this light and effective introductory paragraph from "The Rumor" (1921), we discern such Dreiserisms as "the distinction of being the first" or "an enthusiastic chorus." But these phrases do not determine the tone of the passage. Rather they seem only to suggest that the speaker has risen above them to arrive at the homey observation "everyone was asking himself why no one ever thought of Sam Billings before."

The conversational style of his narration should not lead us to assume, however, that his dialogue is magically closer to the speech of men than other writers. Robert Hazel and other critics err when they suppose that such is the case. In fact, his dialogue is highly stylized. Moreover, it is neither dialectical nor always even idiomatic. One need only compare a passage of black speech from Ellen Glasgow or Faulkner to see how carefully Caldwell avoids strict adherence to the diction and speech patterns of the black. "Nine Dollars Worth of Mumble" (1937) is perhaps his only story about blacks from the point of view of a black narrator: "You couldn't see no stars, you couldn't see no moon, you couldn't see nothing much but a measly handful of sparks on the chimney spout. It was a mighty poor beginning for a courting on a ten o'clock night. Hollering didn't do a bit of good, and stomping up and down did less."

Nor does forthcoming dialogue become noticeably more "realistic" than the language of the narration. Youster Brown demands an effective charm from a "conjur" woman, Sally Lucky, saying: "I'm getting dog-tired of handing you over all my money and not getting no action for it. . . . Look here, now, woman, is you able to do things or ain't you?" This dialogue is in no respect an authentic reproduction of a recognizable black dialect. Rather, it is the same vaguely rural speech Caldwell assigns all his backcountry people. The "is you" and "woman" are enough to suggest black American English, however, in the context of the narration—though the phrase "no action" strikes the ear as patently false. The result might be compared to Hemingway's efforts to convince us we are reading French, Italian, or Spanish. When Youster uneasily asks if Sally's charm might get him "trouble with the law," she replies, loftily: "All my charms and curses are private dealings. . . . As long as you do like I tell you, and keep your mouth shut, you won't have no trouble with the law, I see to that."

While there is certainly an attempt here to sketch black speakers, the effort depends largely upon suggestion rather than faithful reproduction of diction and speech patterns. In the same fashion, by suggestion rather than careful depiction, Caldwell records the speech of his whites as well. Sister Bessie, the illiterate hill woman of *Tobacco Road*, does not speak "realistically" when she says to Jeeter: "It would require a younger man for me to be satisfied. . . . Dude there is just suitable for preaching and living with me."[10] In brief, neither Caldwell's dialogue nor his dialects are as "true-to-life" as many have thought, but both offer what is more important than attempted fidelity: the appearance of reality. The total impression is such that Caldwell need not fear occasional lapses in tone since his characters usually express appropriate sentiments, and the illusion of life remains undisturbed.[11]

Imagery

Measured against his more accomplished contemporaries, Caldwell's imagery at first appears simplistic, but in fact it is as artful as his prose style. Just as he does not experiment daringly with language, being neither studiously literary as Faulkner and Hemingway sometimes are nor defiant of literary conventions, neither does he resort to the sort of complicated web of imagery they used. Whether it is mythic, Freudian (Freudian-Marxist), or biblical, it is invariably elementary. Much of it, in fact, might be called "American biblical" or "fundamental Protestant." To understand it, one needs only a basic knowledge of Christian and, to a lesser extent, Judaic mythology.[12] Will Thompson, as we have earlier seen, was tacitly compared to Christ and his last hours parallel in rough outline those of Christ's last week, as they are reconstructed in the synoptic gospels. Thus the intensity of Caldwell's Christian imagery bears little resemblance to that of his Jewish acquaintance Nathanael West, whose novel of the same year as *God's Little Acre,* the remarkable *Miss Lonelyhearts* (1933), displays a much more comprehensive grasp of Christian thought.[13] Caldwell generally accomplished his goals with a tacit allusion to a few well-known events from the life of Christ.

In the very title of his story "Kneel to the Rising Sun," for example, he resorts to a pun popular in English Christian literature for almost a millennium, the discovery of correspondence between the "sun" and the "son of God." This lynching story (1935) has as its central event an episode suggesting the Crucifixion. It tells the story of two tenant farmers, Lonnie and Clem, the one white, the other black, and their persecution at the hands of their cruel and greedy employer, Arch Gunnard. A well-to-do cotton farmer, Gunnard is as vicious a figure as Caldwell ever drew. His hobby of collecting dogs' tails, cropped with a razor-sharp clasp knife as he sits in the sun before a filling station surrounded by fawning cronies, appalled a whole generation of American readers. The cowing of Lonnie who has come to plead for "rations" is achieved when Arch contemplates his tenant's dog's tail: "I ain't ever seen a hound in all my life that needed a tail that long to hunt rabbits with. It's way too long for just a common, ordinary everyday ketch hound." And then with mock solicitude he asks: ". . . all right with you, ain't it, Lonnie? . . . I don't seem to hear no objections." This horrid episode depends partially for its effect on the Freudian-Marxist imagery that Caldwell frequently uses since the cropping of the dog's tail is clearly equated with the castration of its owner who is deprived of his manhood by the economic exploitation of Gunnard. Nevertheless, it is Christian imagery that dominates the story in which most of Caldwell's strands—including animal imagery—are present.

Clem is a black Christ who walks country roads teaching his disciple Lonnie a religion of social justice. But Lonnie, a composite of Judas and Peter, denies his black master just before dawn and betrays him to armed men, the leader of whom is Arch Gunnard whose name hints at his "gunman's" function in the story. From motives of cowardice and false racial values, Lonnie reveals Clem's hiding place to Arch and his followers, who find the black pressed against a tree high above his persecutors. Lonnie, who hangs back "could see everybody with guns raised, and far into the sky above the sharply outlined face of Clem Henry gleamed in the rising sun. His body was hugging the slender top of the pine." When the bloody body succumbs to volleys of gunfire, the sky turns from gray to red, and the sun appears in a scene of death and transfiguration that might recall Melville's *Billy Budd,* as Lonnie sinks to his knees in horror-stricken recognition of the enormity of the act that has just transpired.

Caldwell's animal imagery plays a large role in the early stories of rural Georgia and northern New England, but it is more easily overlooked than the mythic and theological currents that run through the stories because it seems so naturally a part of country life. Though he can recruit such exotic fauna as a polar bear ("Hamrick's Polar Bear," 1937), most stories offer only chickens, dogs, rabbits, hogs, mules, or horses. The value assigned them varies with any given story, though rabbits are consistently meant to suggest helpless frightened human beings, the prey of every cruel and predatory force the world can boast. In "Molly Cottontail" (1931), a boy's refusal to shoot a rabbit becomes an indictment of the brutality implicit in the code of the southern gentleman and a defense of humanism.

Both "Savannah River Payday" (1931) and "Kneel to the Rising Sun" compare men to animals. In the first story, they are like mules "killed during the past two weeks by heat and overwork at the sawmill," while in the second, exploiters are seen as rapacious "fattening hogs" devouring a half-starved old tenant farmer. In "Savannah River Payday," buzzards, a traditional symbol of the cowardly predator, hover over dead mules waiting for a chance to claw at the rotting flesh. Some moments later we find two white men bringing into town the body of a black killed in an accident at a sawmill. The body is lashed to a running board like a dead deer. In one story after another, Caldwell writes as a naturalist: men and women are beasts and rural Georgia is a dog's world, a *mondo cane,* where women are "flowing bitches" and men are jackass stallions when they are not whipped curs.

The landscape, as we have seen earlier, is both realistic and symbolic in this fiction. Often Caldwell's stories are set in a hellish wasteland where baking heat and dancing fires suggest that his characters are already damned. "Savannah River Payday," a story the squeamish would do well to avoid, is typical in this respect: "The July sun blazed over the earth and shriveled the grass and weeds until they were as dry as crisp autumn leaves. A cloud of dense black smoke blew over from the other side of the river when somebody threw an armful of fat pine on the fire under the moonshine still." The protagonists are torturers who anticipate the horrors of the concentration camp as they knock out the gold teeth of the black they are apparently transporting to an undertaker: "Red pushed the Negro's lips away from the teeth while Jake hammered away at the gold. The sun had made the teeth so hot they burned his fingers when he picked them off the bridge.[14]

As might be expected, Freudian images predominate in stories of sexual awakening and initiation. Two of the best of those are the very early "Midsummer Passion" (1929), Caldwell's first published story, and "A Swell-looking Girl" (1931). Both are humorous and regard the sex drive as an irrational mystery to delight the heart of men rather than the darkly frightening force it sometimes is in both the stories and novels. "A Swell-looking Girl" is the tale of an empty-headed young rustic who foolishly exhibits his pretty new wife to his scapegrace cronies. Lem's pride of conquest and possession leads him to overreach as he lifts his wife's dress to show his friends her delicate good taste in lingerie. In a teasing sequence Caldwell tells us how Lem lifts Ozzie's hem ". . . a little higher and a little higher. . . . The boys crowded closer to Ozzie." The final revelation, of course, is that "Ozzie had nothing on at all under her dress. She was a swell-looking girl, all right." The recognition of a woman solely in terms of her subservience or her private parts is lighthearted here and in "Midsummer Passion," but such is not always the case, and the place of sexuality in a woman's life is never finally resolved in Caldwell's fiction. The language of these stories and the situations described are replete with sexual innuendos apparent to a perceptive reader. Like Willie in "August Afternoon," the short story source of *Journeyman,* Ozzie sat on the edge of the porch "with her legs crossed high." Expressions like "pink thing" or "pink little things" used in the context of such a narration become ambiguous allusions not to the girl's underwear, as the naive narrator believes, but to the intimate flesh, just as the adjective *pinkish* or the more specific term *a female thing* serve a similar function in "Midsummer Passion."

Caldwell's Narrative Point of View and Vaunted "Objectivity"

Caldwell's experimentation with point of view and the long road to strict objectivity were laborious. In his early stories, he often displays a tendency toward sentimentality, and he found it necessary to compensate for it with an exaggerated toughness: " 'Now, tell it.' Gene ground the order between his teeth, pushing the automatic under the man's belt. 'Let's hear everything you know about her—and tell it straight! Get me? Come on, out with it! I want to know everything you know about her.' "[15] The first person narration, he may have believed, seemed likely to generate a sympathy for the narrator that might cloud his objectivity. For this reason, perhaps, many of the earliest stories are told from the third person: *The Bastard* (1929) (from which the excerpt), *Poor Fool* (1930), "Midsummer Passion" (1929), and "The Mating of Marjorie" (1930) are examples. The third person helped to maintain the aesthetic distance he sought. But such a narrative point of view alone could not ensure objectivity: "He was coming—he was coming—God bless him! He was coming to marry her—coming all the way from Minnesota!" Though this story, "The Mating of Marjorie," is not told by the protagonist herself, the excitement and wonder expressed are clearly Marjorie's own.

However, in the midst of these same years, Caldwell seems to have realized that a first person narration need not be susceptible to sentimentality, that the "toughness" of the narrator could be made even more apparent from a first person point of view than from a third. The narrator-speaker might simply react to the horrors about him in a restrained fashion, as here in "Martha Jean" (1935): "Once I thought I heard Martha Jean scream, but when I stopped and listened in the stinging sleet, I could not hear it again. After that I did not know whether it was she or whether it was only the wind that cried against the sharp corners of the buildings." In like fashion the first person speaker might be a naïf, whose observations, though detailed, rarely lead to mature conclusions or whose final judgment must be formulated by the reader because the speaker is insufficiently articulate. After Mark Twain, Sherwood Anderson had enshrined the naive narrator, passing him along to Hemingway, who had himself taken much the same course as Caldwell in developing a point of view. The bafflement of Nick Adams and the "toughness" of Jake Barnes produce the similar effects of absolving the author of the necessity to commit himself. Caldwell further discovered that a certain naiveté enhanced his humorous stories of rural grotesques and that he could maintain a uniform tone, regardless of whether the narration was first or third person.

Thus in "Country Full of Swedes" (1930), Stan tells us without inhibition: "This is the damndest country for unexpected raising of all kinds of unlooked-for hell a man is apt to run across in a lifetime of traveling. If a man's born and raised in the Back Kingdom, he ought to stay there where he belongs; that's what I'd done if I'd had the sense to stay out of this down-country near the Bay, where you don't ever know, God-helping, what's going to happen next, where, or when." At roughly the same time in another story, "The Automobile That Wouldn't Run" (1930), an auctorial voice every bit as exuberant and unself-conscious tells us: "Everybody in the woods had heard about Mal Anderson. He was the best banjo player between Rangely and Caribou, for one thing. And he was one of the best woodsmen ever to lay a tree down in the woods."

But no artifact can ever hide the hand of its artist long, and Caldwell's work is no exception. In the more serious novels he was always obliged to take sides. He simply could not keep himself out of the story entirely by taking advantage either of humor or toughness to achieve distance. It was one thing to look with objectivity at the panty-obsessed rustic of a short story and another to consider the desperate dilemma of a starving tenant farmer in an extended narration. The depth of Caldwell's sympathy for a despairing Jeeter Lester is readily apparent:

> The urge he felt to stir the ground and to plant cotton in it, and after that to sit in the shade during the hot months watching the plants sprout and grow, was even greater than the pains of hunger in his stomach. He could sit calmly and bear the feeling of hunger, but to be compelled to live and look each day at the unplowed fields was an agony he believed he could not stand many more days.
>
> His head dropped forward on his knees, and sleep soon overcame him and brought a peaceful rest to his tired heart and body. [16]

Many of Caldwell's "Depression" stories are in fact baldly propagandistic, and he was often criticized by purists for interrupting the narrative of *Tobacco Road* in chapter 7 to attack sharecropping in a set speech and to urge collectivism. The single tenable rationale for such behavior is that Caldwell's objectivity is no greater than other careful writers, but that his taut prose and his failure to intrude when recording the violent acts so much a part of southern writing have won him that reputation.

A consideration for a moment of *Georgia Boy* might reveal a contrast, however, to the partisan display of sympathies discernible in *Tobacco Road, God's Little Acre,* and other books and stories. This "novel" was published after Caldwell had established a reputation for merciless objectivity and, moreover, provides a naive first person nar-

rator. The biggest difference between William Stroup (the Georgia
boy of about twelve who tells the story) and Huck Finn or Holden
Caulfield—apart from his less inquiring mind—is William's role of
observer rather than participator. In *Georgia Boy* things happen to Pa
Stroup and Handsome Brown, the teenaged black "yard boy," not to
William. In fact, William's part is to tell us what happened and let
us decide.

The stories of *Georgia Boy,* for the most part, are extraordinarily
slight. That is not to say that familiar topics such as the sex drive
and racial injustice are altogether ignored. They are not; but they are
touched on in such a manner as to escape the serious attention they
command in more substantial works. Caldwell seems here to be attempting a *jeu d'esprit* to demonstrate his versatility. He wants to
show that he need not always perform in the expected fashion. It is
the same urge that drove him to broadcasting or, much later on, to
juvenile literature.

Georgia Boy began as a story entitled "My Old Man," and like
Hemingway's story of the same title, it shows considerable debt to
Sherwood Anderson. In all the stories of this "novel," we find a
youthful confusion about adult sex drives and dishonesty, though,
again, far less seriously or pointedly treated than in the other two
writers. Most specifically, *Georgia Boy* is indebted to the endemic idea
of those near-contemporaries that the company of men is more edi-
fying and cleaner than that of women, that women corrupt and destroy the candid interaction of males. All women are either viragoes
of the wash pot or social circle or, worse yet, beautiful lazy schemers
who lure men away from their sons. William mildly resents the fact
that his father comes home drunk with a young woman; but once his
mother has driven the youthful *arriviste* into the night to do battle
and Pa has locked the door on them both, William tells us confiden-
tially, "It sure felt good being there in the dark with him."[17]

Sex for itself does not interest William at all. He never overtly
comments on a woman's desirability. Rather, he regards women as
objects of curiosity or, more often, troublemakers ready to provide
difficulties for his all-too-fallible father: "I had forgotten all about Ma
because I was so busy listening to Mrs. Weatherbee and watching my
old man [The "grass widow" is giggling furiously as Morris Stroup
tickles her toes with a chicken feather], but just then I looked across
the yard and saw Ma coming. She made straight for the porch where
they were." (William had come to warn his father but had forgotten

his mission). The great weakness of this point of view is that it becomes an academic exercise. There is no reason for it. It exists only for effect, and that effect sometimes collapses since many of the stories are so unlikely, so "unrealistic." Minimum caricature rather than maximum must characterize the child's point of view, as most readers of the "ending" of *Huckleberry Finn* will sadly acknowledge. Huck, Holden, and George Willard have an eye for detail and are literal, but they are sensitive as well. William Stroup is more like a camera who accords equal importance to everything in range. In other words, the book's objectivity, in its unfavorable sense, becomes overwhelming. Caldwell, we must conclude, worked better in the novels with a limited omniscient third person.

Even his growing concern for racial justice grows dulled by the point of view assumed in the stories that make up *Georgia Boy*. Young William Stroup seems to find irrationality something of a virtue. At least he records tolerantly his father's wildest schemes to make money baling paper or collecting scrap iron. But he watches with similar equanimity the outrages performed against his friend Handsome Brown. For this reason Handsome Brown never attains a dignity remotely similar to that of Twain's Nigger Jim. The abused black teenager, kept in virtual servitude by the parents of his "friend," may often insist on a more rational mode of behavior than that practiced by the "white folks," but he never takes on the dimensions of a spiritual adviser as Jim does, nor does he, despite his color, show a kinship to Caldwell's "natural man." His unprotesting presence serves to show, of course, that racism even in its most benign and comic form is a detestable custom. However, William's wordless acceptance of the treatment Handsome Brown receives works against Caldwell's intention.

One of many instances of this failure might be seen in the short story-chapter "The Time Handsome Brown Ran Away." Here Handsome finds employment as a human target at a carnival after he has abandoned the Stroups because Pa Stroup has stolen his only possession, a banjo, and sold it for a dollar. Pa finds him at his carnival booth and, to encourage him to return home, pays for the use of six baseballs.

Pa turned loose with a fast one that caught Handsome square in the forehead before he could dodge out of the way. Handsome was so surprised he didn't know what had happened. He sat down on the ground and rubbed his head until the man in the red silk shirt ran back to find out if anything serious had happened to him. Presently Handsome got up, staggering just a little, and stuck his head through the round hole once more.[18]

The tone of unprotesting acceptance conveyed here by William Stroup suggests not so much that Caldwell is manfully holding his anger in check, but that the vacant narrator might in time be capable of the same conduct as his father. Perhaps in this case Caldwell's un-friendly critics are finally right. The "objectivity" of *Georgia Boy* is too pronounced to be truly effective.

Chapter Seven
A Final Assessment

Popularity

Caldwell has so often been accused of serving Mammon, of writing solely for the dollar, that the charge deserves some examination.[1] But even the briefest survey of his work will demonstrate the injustice and exaggeration of such an accusation. More than half of his twenty-eight novels, for example, were written at periods when there was little demand for his work, either before he had won an audience or after that audience had waned. At least three of his novels appear to have been privately printed at his own expense, *The Bastard, Poor Fool,* and *The Sacrilege of Alan Kent,* and one was never published, "The Bogus Ones." The first two of these he could ill afford to publish, and though money was more plentiful by the publication date of *The Sacrilege of Alan Kent,* he would certainly have known by then that it was not the sort of book Americans would buy.

It is concomitantly said that he tried to produce too much work, that he was in some respects a one-man industry. To this charge there is a grain of truth, but here again the motive never seems to have been mercenary. Caldwell worked furiously both at the start of his career and after his name had begun to be known, but he never markedly increased his publication rate after achieving popular acclaim. Approximately 65 percent of his total output of short stories were written before 1940, many of which were published before he had achieved even a modicum of fame—or notoriety—and fully 80 percent were in print by 1950 when his popular reputation was still secure.

To be sure, when success came, Caldwell grew eager to exact generous payment for his writing and for his time. He sometimes charged fees for interviews, for example, and he always drove a hard bargain for his fiction. But some of these practices existed only to discourage the frivolous and to provide him the undisturbed writing hours he needed after he had become widely known. Also he seems to have been convinced that large royalties were the identifying feature of a good writer, a version, perhaps, of the Protestant success ethic his Calvinist family had never scorned. He was well aware, too, of what sort of demands impressed the front office at Scribner's or Viking, and he did not intend to take a back seat to Ernest Hemingway, Thomas Wolfe, or William Faulkner if he could avoid it. Moreover, the modest circumstances of his youth seemed to have spurred him on to the honest accumulation of wealth.

In the busiest periods of his life, he accepted such commissions as the editorship of *American Folkways*, which could in no way remunerate him as his fiction could. He experimented with great success in a new genre, the photo-essay with Margaret Bourke-White, and he undertook a host of journalistic and radio assignments to satisfy his curiosity about Eastern Europe and the furious tempest brewing overseas. Yet he must have known that these could never gain him the literary recognition he craved since leaving the South for New England or provide him the income of a *God's Little Acre*.

Artistic Integrity

He never disparaged certain pieces of his own writing as mere hackwork, as Faulkner and Fitzgerald did theirs. He never confessed to writing less honestly for a mass market than he had written from 1930 to 1933, when he was publishing stories in the critically demanding little magazines. Indeed, this idea seems never to have occurred to him. Nor, like Joseph Hergesheimer, did he ever seem to fear the toll that popular taste might take on his fiction.[2] Instead, after the success of *God's Little Acre*, he relied on his instinct and continued writing as he wished. He wrote quickly, perhaps too quickly, though he did not so much increase the production he had maintained from 1929 to 1933 as continue it. He recognized no such distinction between "serious fiction" and "commercial fiction" as that defined by Ronald E. Martin in his competent and well-written study of Hergesheimer, an American whose earlier career bears distinct resemblances to Caldwell's:

Serious fiction . . . ideally has no . . . inducements to the writer to do less than his best. The "serious" novel or story develops according to the author's own view of life and according to the standards inherent in the work itself. Thus it has a certain autonomy, uniqueness, and integrity lacked by a work produced for the marketplace, and is able to discover to its reader more about himself and the world than would be possible if the reader's own expectations and prejudices were held sancrosanct.[3]

Caldwell never pandered his craft for money. He understood that his audience—intellectual or popular, it made no difference to him— wanted a rousing story; but he refused to provide the traditional fodder of the popular writer, an adventure story. He offered lineal plots which were episodic and anecdotal. He sought to entertain and to hold, using the tried methods of the storyteller to achieve these not ignominious ends. In short, he wrote as well as he could, according to his own standards.

Ultimately he was always more interested in characters than in plot, however. But, here too, he demanded freedom to draw not the "idealizations of the reader's self,"[4] so often sought in popular fiction, nor flat figures who change their characters at a moment's notice.[5] For example, in the final pages of *Gone with the Wind,* Scarlett O'Hara suddenly realizes she never loved Ashley Wilkes but only the fantasy she wove about him. And character reversals come by the score in *Uncle Tom's Cabin,* as nearly everyone pauses to change heart. This instant-reversal syndrome has long marred even the work of popular writers of genius like Dickens, whose Nancy Sikes, old Martin Chuzzlewit, old Mr. Dombey, and even Pip provide examples. Max Brand, who like Caldwell sold millions of copies, indeed confessed, "The basic formula I use is simple; good man turns bad, bad man turns good."[6]

Caldwell's most memorable characters, on the other hand, are consistently, even stubbornly undeviating. While this in itself is not necessarily a virtue, it does tend to bring them closer to life than those figures of popular fiction whose melodramatic changes and "realizations" come at the drop of a hat. Self-knowledge is a rare attainment in Caldwell's world: Jeeter Lester dies unenlightened; Ty Ty Walden's recognition of Will Thompson's vision cannot liberate him from fruitless delving in the earth; even Will Thompson himself or Lorene Horey seem uncertain why they behave as they do in resisting an oppression they vaguely understand. Genuine recognition of one's motives, not to speak of change of heart, comes rarely into one's life, Caldwell has seen; and he is satisfied if his readers begin to fathom what his characters so often miss.

The finest American fiction since Hawthorne has always acknowledged the dreary fact that self-discovery remains beyond the reach of most. Huck Finn's decision to light out for the Territory, we may recall, is made only after he has tested a score of characters by the yardstick of Christian charity. Even then he has doubtless learned less about himself and the world about him than we who are privileged to look over his shoulder. And Lambert Strether is still not clear as to what he must do after his prolonged sojourn in Paris, though he has definite ideas of what befits Chad.

Such praise, however, must not raise Caldwell beyond his deserts, for his books after 1944 too often contain figures indistinguishable from those of the ephemeral best seller. He came to rely mechanically on devices he had used skillfully years earlier, such as partial identification of figures by a characteristic remark in the manner of Dickens, or on the "exciting force": a new character designed to infuse life into the narration. With Bessie Rice, the self-ordained preacher woman of *Tobacco Road,* and Will Thompson, the obsessed labor agitator of *God's Little Acre,* he succeeded admirably in rousing his stories from incipient lethargy. But even these fine novels, we may recall, contain characters obviously meant to serve a similar function, like Pluto Swint or Lov Bensey, whose promising first appearances come to little. Moreover, after *Georgia Boy,* Caldwell sometimes succumbed to the best-seller contagion and created slickly protean figures whose characters shifted predictably to accommodate auctorial pleasure.

Caldwell and Formulaic Fiction

In *Golden Multitudes,* Frank Luther Mott claims that "about one eighth of our best sellers employ exotic settings."[7] In this number he is certainly including the myriad of historical novels that deluged the country in the thirties and forties, beginning with Hervey Allen's *Anthony Adverse,* published the same year as *God's Little Acre* but by far a more successful book in its popular reception. But Mott is careful to distinguish degrees of exoticism. Thus the Svengali-ridden Paris of George du Maurier's *Trilby* (1895) "was exotic to its readers, while that of *The Razor's Edge* [Maugham's big success of 1944] was not."[8] Mott's distinction points out the difficulty of ever determining what constitutes the "exotic." Certainly Hemingway's European locales were not exactly terra incognita, but few would deny their attraction for two generations of American readers. The fiction of the Southern Renaissance showed that the modern South was every bit as seductive to readers of Faulkner, Robert Penn Warren, and William Styron as the magnolia-scented land they debunked. And American theater audiences found the neighborhood of *Tobacco Road* as grotesque, strange, and different as any they had ever encountered, Al Capp admitting that much of his inspiration for *Li'l Abner* came from the Kirkland staging of *Tobacco Road*. Caldwell's South, then, was exotic enough for a popular audience that may not have discerned that it was also a highly imaginative landscape, where summer heat and the smell of fires are as meaningful as the highly charged turbulent winds that whistle through *Wuthering Heights*.

Stylistically, writers of popular fiction tread a narrow path, regarding innovation with horror. Herman Wouk or Taylor Caldwell do not experiment. The language of the popular novel in its syntax, diction, and level of abstraction tends to be determined by readability or governed by the same demand for simplicity that controls structure and characterization. Caldwell did not stray in this respect, though once or twice he superficially imitated Faulkner's use of italics in narration or introduced unidentified speakers by enclosing their comments in parentheses and quotation marks. Neither of these devices will strike the reader as either organic or inventive. In general, however, Caldwell's movement toward a conversational prose—or at least the appearance of it—will pass muster in any review of American realistic writing in the last fifty years. If his dialogue contains repetitions, non sequiturs, and logical cul de sacs, or if he began by avoiding subordinate clauses, then so did his model Hemingway, who received a Nobel Prize for a "style-forming mastery of the art of modern narration." Both writers have stated publicly their belief in the value of a simple diction. Caldwell agrees wholeheartedly with Hemingway's conclusion that American writers before them "did not use the words that people have always used in speech."

The drollery and slapstick of his writing has undoubtedly contributed much to endearing Caldwell to a mass audience, for the reader of popular fiction has historically been attracted by humor. Perhaps as important was his timeliness and topicality, often an important criterion in popular fiction. A glance at the American best-seller list, from Harriet Beecher Stowe's *Uncle Tom's Cabin* to Jacqueline Susann's *Valley of the Dolls,* will show that a current issue or problem (slavery, drugs) can contribute to the success of the popular book. Caldwell began by trying to write tough city crime stories in the vein of Dashiell Hammett and Raymond Chandler. Until 1944 most of his work featured timely settings of the Depression-ridden South. Yet it is important to remember that his largest sales came not in the original years of publication but much later. Depression readers, like Depression moviegoers, were not especially attracted to fictional representation of current plights. Escapist froth was the order of the day in the popular arts, like Edna Ferber's runaway best seller *Cimarron*, the year after the Wall Street crash. Of course, in presenting sexual themes with great frankness, Caldwell was certainly both timely and widely appealing. From *Tobacco Road* he had large numbers of readers seeking only titillation in his pages, though numerous others were directed to Caldwell's treatment of sexual themes by the example of a world literature already engrossed in a more honest depiction of physical passion than had hitherto existed.

Yet novels offer more meaning to some readers than to others. Some obviously read Caldwell for his sex, just as some read Hemingway for his adventure or love stories and Nabokov's *Lolita* for its shocking subject (though the sophomoric once thought they had discovered a sustained allegory or a roman á clef). Even to the more serious, Caldwell was often nothing more than a simple storyteller with a gift for faithful portrayal of the primitives he saw about him. Relatively few recognized his studied disingenuousness, and they failed to gauge its depth. Like the still-life painter, Caldwell deceives us not only in his apparently naive choice of subject matter but in the artful arrangement of his characters, themes, and situations. His world, however, is actually as complicated as Faulkner's, whose grotesqueries and gothic horrors serve a purpose much like Caldwell's. And his vision remains essentially a dark one, though he has protested a too-gloomy interpretation of his work, insisting that he means to strike a happy balance.

Caldwell's work, then, both resembles and differs from that of the popular, successful writer. Chiefly, he enjoys a freedom denied the latter. He seeks not just to win an audience—perhaps the greatest concern of popular fiction—but to change one. In maintaining his intellectual independence, in keeping a possessive control over his writing, he is ready to affront reader and critic alike. Though he offers the general reader enough popular "ingredients" to satisfy his taste, these elements are bent to the service of an artistic vision.

Caldwell's Place Today

If Caldwell did not lack praise by such earlier critics as Malcolm Cowley, Kenneth Burke, Joseph Warren Beach, and Joseph Wood Krutch, today his stature may more accurately be measured by the neglect he suffers. He is without any question a minor writer, and further, a limited one. Philosophically he is of few ideas and those often inconsistent. He has never decided whether it is the heart or the head to which he owes the greater allegiance. His belief in feeling, intuition, and emotion as God-directed often falters when opposed by the strong pressure of a naturalistic determinism that also guides his thought. About sexual passion he is simultaneously knowledgeable and as innocent as Steve Henderson, the wooden sixteen-year-old of *Summertime Island* (1968), a typical late attempt based on a short story written more than three decades earlier.

His work of the past twenty-five years has shown that he does not really understand the human beings he writes about, a more serious fault than being unable to depict them vividly or to tell their stories in felicitous prose. This, regrettably, is perhaps the most devastating criticism one can level against a writer. *Love and Money* (1954), *Gretta* (1955), *Jenny by Nature* (1961), *The Weather Shelter* (1969), *Annette* (1973), and the other novels issued from Caldwell's too-productive hand are shades of a declined talent. The plots wander erratically, the prose—always graceless, though deadly effective American plain style at one time—has become petrified:

I had been so startled when Aunt Rosemary woke me up in the middle of the night and began whispering to me that I did not realize how close she was to me until I felt the softness of her body through her thin nightgown and could see the whole fullness of her large round breasts in the dim light. I had a sudden stiffening of my body and felt a throbbing urge for her body and wished she had been Bonnie or some other girl I could hug in my arms.[9]

Though this is tame stuff for the late sixties, it reflects Caldwell's lifelong fascination with "sexual awakening," now reduced to a labored "pocketbook" style and, more regretfully, "pocketbook" mentality.

However, it is not the purpose of this study to denigrate a writer of Caldwell's achievement anymore than it has been to promote him undeserved. Previous chapters have shown the strong quality of his finest work. But we must always remember that to go beyond that small canon of several short novels and a dozen or so short stories is unrewarding.

In the history of American literature Caldwell belongs prominently to the list of also-rans, primarily on the basis of *Tobacco Road* and *God's Little Acre*. But an enduring interest in both of these fine novels raises him above writers who might otherwise be judged his peers. For this reason it is difficult to compare him with others, either American or foreign. Nevertheless the temptation understandably remains to do just that. As much as he varies in other respects, his reputation is like that of certain inspired popular writers of the last century, like Anatole France or Frederick Marryat, or, perhaps, in this century, like Erich Maria Remarque whose accomplished early novels promised a future that never escaped best sellerdom. In his own country and time, comparisons are harder yet.

Like his mentor Sherwood Anderson, he is known today for one or two books, but unlike Anderson, Caldwell was not really a pioneer or a discoverer. The career of Caldwell's friend John Steinbeck who continued to write and win accord after his talent had declined offers parallels to Caldwell's own. A better comparison might be made with Ralph Ellison, or perhaps, James Jones, each of whom has established a minor, if respectable reputation on the basis of a single compelling book; or with the once popular and esteemed J. P. Marquand, much as his understated social satires vary from Caldwell's two-fisted assaults on conscience and funny bone; or with Jack London who actually led the flamboyant life Caldwell seemed to from his book jackets: "[Caldwell] worked his way through the University of Virginia and Pennsylvania, graduating from neither. For a time he held a variety of jobs, working as a mill laborer, cotton-picker, hack-driver, stagehand, reporter, cook and waiter. Exactly six feet tall, he has the physique of a football pro (another job he held) and a round, candid, innocent face." Like London, Caldwell suffered a hopeless confusion between romantic notions and naturalistic conventions, half-believing, too, in the male brute who alone could tame and hold the most desirable female. Caldwell also wrote speedily and tirelessly. And if London staked out a special area in fiction for himself, the adventure story inside a naturalistic framework, then so did Caldwell in portraying a baking Georgia where logic falters and men and women behave like the children we know them to be.

In the chapter "Sounds" from *Walden,* Thoreau hears the eerie call of an owl and remarks that owls serve us well: "I rejoice that there are owls. Let them do the idiotic and maniacal hooting for man. They represent . . . the stark twilight and unsatisfied thoughts which all men have." Caldwell, too, sounds such a maniacal hoot for all of us, not one of derision, but of wild recognition of the irrational and dark. Ultimately, he seems to say, everyone is a Georgia boy standing in a dusty yard, squinting out over quivering rows of stunted cotton in the July sun. Caldwell's achievement is modest, but it is good that he lived and wrote.

Notes and References

Chapter One

1. Caldwell's birthdate usually is given as 1903, but he has admitted privately to being born in 1902.
2. Erskine Caldwell, *Call It Experience* (New York, 1951), p. 25.
3. R. J. Gray makes a similar point in his article "Southwestern Humor, Erskine Caldwell, and the Comedy of Frustrations", *Southern Literary Journal* 8, no. 1 (Fall 1975):3–26.
4. Caldwell, *Experience*, p. 30.
5. Ibid., p. 35.
6. Linda Arret, reference assistant to the Alderman Library of the University of Virginia, has written me, however, that "Caldwell was registered from September 1923, until 21 April 1927, when he left school. He was not awarded a degree."
7. The atmosphere of the *Journal* was not altogether hostile toward creative writing, however. See Caldwell, *Experience*, p. 31.
8. This is not to say that he never made use of naive narrators. In the vein of Hemingway, he, too, wrote Anderson-like stories. But as Shields McIlwaine notes, "These sex stories, however, with the pathetic note of adolescence about them are not in Caldwell's characteristic vein—a vein which is marked by drollery and what Horace Gregory calls 'idiotic gravity' " (*The Southern Poor-White from Lubberland to Tobacco Road* [Norman, Okla., 1939,] p. 225). In *Georgia Boy,* a novel based on short story materials, Caldwell returned to the naive narrator with some success.
9. McIlwaine, *The Southern Poor-White,* p. 227. See also Guy Owen, " 'The Bogus Ones': A Lost Erskine Caldwell Novel," *Southern Library Journal* 11 (1978):39. Owen writes that Caldwell's unpublished novel "The Bogus Ones" contains a "sex scene in which the couple has a witness . . . [a situation] which became a trademark of Caldwell's sex scenes with Lov and Ellie May and Dude and Sister Bessie in *Tobacco Road* and a number of similar episodes in *God's Little Acre, Journeyman,* and *Tragic Ground,* to cite only a few examples."
10. See Note 9. In his article, Owen evaluates the novel which exists now only in "a xeroxed copy of the manuscript . . . given to the D. H. Hill Library at North Carolina State University by the author's first wife, Helen Caldwell Cushman, along with a collection of unpublished poems and several volumes of non-fiction."

11. According to Caldwell, Perkins saw one or two of his stories in the little magazines and wrote him in the autumn of 1929 to inquire if he could see some unpublished ones. Perkins may also have seen, of course, *The New American Caravan,* published in October 1929, that contained "Midsummer Passion." At any rate, F. Scott Fitzgerald did, and he recommended Caldwell to Perkins in January of 1930. For a fuller account of this episode, see my short article, "Fitzgerald's Discovery of Erskine Caldwell," *Fitzgerald/Hemingway Annual 1978* (Detroit: Gale Research Co.), pp. 101–3.

12. See Guy Owen, "Erskine Caldwell's Unpublished Poems," *South Atlantic Bulletin* 43 (May 1978):53–57. Owen offers a brief account of Caldwell's early ambitions as a poet and an overview of some two dozen poems in "xeroxed typescript" in the North Carolina State University Library, which escaped the immolation.

13. Caldwell, *Experience,* p. 163.

14. Malcolm Cowley,—*And I Worked at the Writer's Trade* (New York, 1978), p. 116.

15. Ibid.

16. *God's Little Acre,* it might be recalled, is favorite reading aboard the *Reluctant* in Thomas Heggen's *Mister Roberts.* Ensign Pulver is credited with having read the novel twelve times and being able to recite "certain passages . . . flawlessly."

17. Caldwell, *Experience,* p. 35.

18. Ibid., p. 58

19. Ibid., p. 232.

20. Ibid., p. 108.

21. John M. Bradbury, *Renaissance in the South* (Chapel Hill, 1963), p. 16.

22. Ibid.

23. Erskine Caldwell, *Jackpot* (New York, 1940), p. 331.

24. Ibid., p. 243.

25. Caldwell, *Experience,* p. 235.

26. Erskine Caldwell, "Naturalism and the American Novel," tape recording (Tucson: McGraw-Hill Sound Seminars, 1950).

27. Joseph Warren Beach, *American Fiction: 1920–1940* (New York, 1941), p. 223.

28. Andrew Turnbull, ed., *The Letters of F. Scott Fitzgerald* (New York, 1963), p. 230.

29. Caldwell, *Experience,* p. 238.

Chapter Two

1. Robert Cantwell, *The Humorous Side of Erskine Caldwell* (New York: 1951), p. xix.

2. W.M. Frohock, *The Novel of Violence in America* (Dallas, 1957), p. 121.

3. Malcolm Cowley, "Naturalism in American Literature," in *Evolutionary Thought in America,* ed. Stow Persons (New York: George Braziller, 1956), pp. 326–28.

4. John M. Bradbury, *Renaissance in the South* (Chapel Hill, N.C., 1963), p. 79.

5. Donald W. Heiney, *Contemporary Literature* (Great Neck, N.Y.: Barron's Educational Series, 1954), p. 147.

6. See Bertolt Brecht, "Alienation Effects in Chinese Acting," in *Brecht on Theatre,* trans. and ed. John Willet (New York, 1964), p. 91.

7. Cowley, "Naturalism," p. 332.

8. Cantwell, *Humorous Side,* p. xxii.

Chapter Three

1. More accurately, Caldwell was at this time the author of four unread short novels. *The Bastard* (1929) and *Poor Fool* (1930) had attracted no attention. The Maine novel *(A Lamp for Nightfall)* would remain unpublished for twenty years. Professor Guy Owen has now discovered another novel from this period, hitherto unknown. See " 'The Bogus Ones': A Lost Erskine Caldwell Novel," *Southern Literary Journal* 11 (Fall 1978). Caldwell seems never to have referred publicly to "The Bogus Ones," an unprinted work of some 127 pages, "completed before June 2, 1930." Though faintly autobiographical and concerned with "the plight of the artist in a materialistic society," "The Bogus Ones" has also as a theme New England provincialism and intolerance, an idea also expressed in his Maine novel and prominent in his Yale Review Award for Fiction (1933) short story, "Country Full of Swedes," written probably in 1932.

2. Caldwell sometimes seemed to enjoy playing the role of a cultural noble savage, possibly from a combination of motives: as a defense against the inadequacy of a limited education and as a subtle emphasis of his considerable achievement. Despite frequent claims to ignorance of literature, he has casually admitted to owning a first edition of Dreiser's *Sister Carrie* and to having greatly enjoyed Faulkner's *As I Lay Dying.* In addition, Caldwell has, at one time or another, confessed to a modest knowledge of almost every major American writer in the period from the end of World War I to the decade after World War II.

3. Frank Norris, "Zola as a Romantic Writer," in *The Literary Criticism of Frank Norris,* ed. Donald Pizer (Austin: University of Texas, 1964), p. 71.

4. More than one reader has wondered if Ty Ty's dream of buried gold owed any debt to Faulkner's "Lizards in Jamshyd's Courtyard," *Satur-*

day Evening Post 104 (27 February 1932). In Faulkner's story—later revised for *The Hamlet* (1940)—Flem Snopes deliberately "plants" gold on the Old Frenchman's Place. An even more teasing question might be that of the relation of the visit to a brothel in *Tobacco Road* by Jeeter, Dude, and Bessie who believe it to be a hotel to a similar visit by rustics under the same misconception in Faulkner's *Sanctuary*, published in February 1931, when Caldwell was in the middle of writing his novel.

5. This experimental and highly poetic odyssey of youth was apparently begun in 1928. It appeared in three parts "as the final section of the original edition of *American Earth*, though it was eliminated from subsequent editions of that collection." It was privately printed again in 1936. See Scott MacDonald, "An Evaluative Check-List of Erskine Caldwell's Short Fiction," *Studies in Short Fiction* 15 (Winter 1978):88. In a recent article, "Erskine Caldwell's Unpublished Poems," *South Atlantic Bulletin* 43 (May 1978), Guy Owen reminds us that Caldwell had early ambitions as a poet. Owen writes: "Finally, he [Caldwell] sent a group [of poems] to Louis Untermeyer for an expert's opinion. When Untermeyer wrote him that his poems were no better and no worse than those of thousands of other young Americans, Caldwell accepted his advice to go into another field of writing" (p. 53).

6. Will's delight in being a part of the noisy mill where he works bare-chested and where he "belongs" will remind the reader of the early expressionistic scenes in O'Neill's *The Hairy Ape* (1922). O'Neill himself was undoubtedly influenced by Continental expressionism, which, in turn, had absorbed from earlier Italian futurism the ideas of the aggressive male, the infatuation with machinery, the disregard for all tradition, and the worship of noise and activity. Will Thompson might well have been a disciple of Fillippo Tommaso Marinetti had he been a fin de siècle reader of *Le Figaro* instead of a Georgia weaver.

7. John Steinbeck, *The Grapes of Wrath* (New York: The Viking Press, 1939), p. 204.

8. This theme of awakening, whether to sexual awareness or simply to a realization of human interdependence, is common to many of the naturalists. The simultaneous detachment and awareness of brotherhood that Griselda experiences parallels that of George Willard, felt in his walk through the alleys of the working-class neighborhood of Winesburg in "An Awakening," from *Winesburg, Ohio*. There is a similar account in Thomas Wolfe's *Look Homeward, Angel* (1929).

9. James Korges, *Erskine Caldwell* (Minneapolis, 1969), p. 25.

10. Erskine Caldwell, *Journeyman* (New York, 1935), p. 181.

Chapter Four

1. "August Afternoon" was republished in *We Are the Living* (New York, 1933), the same year it appeared in the first *Esquire*.

2. Erskine Caldwell, *Jackpot* (New York, 1940), p. 331; hereafter page references are cited in the text.

3. Caldwell's language and his use of myth resemble Faulkner's of about the same period. Faulkner, for example, employs the same interweaving of comedy and myth constantly in the "Eula" section of *The Hamlet*, published in 1940, but written in these years. We might notice the similarity of situation and mythocomic overtone in the description of Will Varner's tryst with the wife of one of his tenants: ". . . she would meet him in the afternoon, on pretense of hunting hen-nests, in a thicket beside the creek near her house, in which sylvan Pan-hallowed retreat, the fourteen-year-old boy whose habit it was to spy on them told, Varner would not even remove his hat" (p. 142).

4. R. W. B. Lewis, afterword to *The Confidence Man* by Herman Melville (New York: New American Library, 1964), p. 262.

5. Ibid.

6. George Becker, ed., *Documents of Modern Literary Realism* (Princeton, 1963), p. 19.

7. Robert Hazel, "Notes on Erskine Caldwell," in *Southern Renascence*, ed. L. D. Rubin and R. D. Jacobs (Baltimore, 1966), p. 323.

8. Erskine Caldwell, *A Lamp for Nightfall* (New York, 1952), p. 92.

9. The photo-essays that Caldwell prepared with Margaret Bourke-White provide splendid illustrations of how a landscape or scene can be at once realistic and symbolic. Her photographic talent reflects the ability Caldwell had to define reality through imaginative use of the grotesque. *You Have Seen Their Faces* (1937) contains a number of highly imaginative photographic compositions of rural fundamentalist services of blacks and whites.

10. H.L. Mencken, *The Vintage Mencken* (New York: Vintage Books, 1959), p. 68.

11. Erskine Caldwell, *Deep South* (New York, 1969), p. 51.

12. In addition to publishing *Journeyman* in 1935, however, he saw appear *Kneel to the Rising Sun*, a collection of stories, some of which contain themes of social protest, and *Tenant Farmer*, a biting, nonfiction indictment of southern agricultural serfdom.

13. Caldwell, *You Have Seen Their Faces*, p. 40.

14. On wagering one's wife and gambling with the devil, see Stith Thompson, *Motif Index of Folk Literature*, vol. 5, N2.6, N3, and N4 (Bloomington: Indiana University Press, 1955).

15. It seems likely that Caldwell wrote *Journeyman* in great haste and frequently paid little attention in plotting to the finer details of motivation, a habit that he had established as early as his first novel, but that grew more flagrant later. An example of such a lapse in one of his best books would be the return of Griselda to Scottsville with Pluto, Darling Jill, Rosamond, and Will, after her husband has ranted all morning against Will. One might recall in Caldwell's defense that Faulkner, too, is frequently guilty of non sequiturs and a variety of other lapses. In attempting to motivate

Popeye in *Sanctuary,* a novel that offers its resemblance to *Journeyman,* he appended a chapter that has baffled readers for five decades.

16. Erskine Caldwell, *God's Little Acre* (New York, 1933), p. viii.

17. Maurice Edgar Coindreau, *The Time of William Faulkner: A French View of Modern American Literature,* ed. and trans. George McMillan Reeves with a foreword by Michael Gresset (Columbia: University of South Carolina, 1971).

18. Erskine Caldwell, *Trouble in July* (New York, 1940), p. 191.

19. Erskine Caldwell, *Tobacco Road* (New York, 1932), p. 223.

20. In attempting to depict the black as sexually harmless, no threat to the white man or woman, Caldwell is perhaps intimidated by public opinion. It is the only instance that I can think of when he has compromised his artistic integrity. Even here, it is zeal to protect the black that drives him to invent a character who is unconvincingly pious. He has done what Harriet Beecher Stowe did with Uncle Tom.

Chapter Five

1. These figures are based on those provided by the *World Almanac 1941,* which in turn are taken from the *Negro Year Book* of Tuskegee Institute, edited by Monroe N. Work.

2. W. M. Frohock, *The Novel of Violence in America, 1920–1950* (Dallas, 1957), p. 108.

3. Beach, *American Fiction, 1920–1940,* p. 227.

4. Ibid., p. 247.

5. To be sure, a few black faces people the background.

6. Walter Allen, *The Modern Novel in Britain and the United States* (New York: 1964), p. 112.

7. Throughout this work, I have deliberately used the Joycean expression *epiphany,* because it is so intimately associated with modern fiction, especially the short story. But Aristotle's term *peripiteia* or even *discovery* or *revelation* are perhaps as good. Maxwell Anderson, who identified *peripiteia* with *discovery,* wrote in *Off Broadway* (New York: Wm. Sloane Associates, 1947), p. 59, that the central crisis of a tragedy "should consist in a discovery by the leading character which has an indelible effect on this thought and emotion and completely alters his course of action." Although many Caldwell stories, like Sherwood Anderson's, often display just such a discovery, others, the best ones, tend to shift the discovery from the protagonist to the reader.

8. Beach, *American Fiction: 1920–1940,* p. 245.

Chapter Six

1. Hartmut Heuermann, *Erskine Caldwells Short Stories* (Frankfurt/Main, 1974), p. 19. Heuermann, whose contention is that Caldwell must

be considered a short story writer exclusively, considers the weaknesses of his novels in regard to handling of time and loose episodic construction of plots to be a failure—in Heuermann's eyes—to create characters who embody the myths and thought of their time and concludes: "The manifest shortcomings in Caldwell's novels . . . become virtues in the short stories." He writes further: "The fact that his novels rarely exceed two hundred pages—and, in fact, most fall short of this length—is an outward indication of the inner disposition of his creative talent: Caldwell tends to the short form in literature; he is a master of the short story." *(Er ist ein Meister der Kurzgeschichte.)* While Heuermann's case may be slightly overstated—consider the title of his book—his arguments are cogent, and his case for Caldwell's preference for short fiction is indisputable.

2. I have not felt it appropriate or necessary to comment on the personality of Caldwell. But careful study of Margaret Bourke-White's autobiography, of Caldwell's own statements, and of vast quantities of material written about him in the popular press in the thirties and forties leads one to conclude that his cautious shyness, not to mention suspicious temperament, proceeds from a certain insecurity.

3. From a letter to Henry Brevoort, 11 December 1824, by Washington Irving. Reprinted in *The Dimensions of the Short Story* (New York, Dodd, Mead & Co., 1966), p. 518.

4. Here I must disagree with Heuermann who describes Caldwell as opposite to Faulkner in the respect that the latter's "short stories always point to a recognizable tendency to the epic dimensions of the novels" *(Erskine Caldwells Short Stories,* p. 19).

5. "Masses of Men" published in 1933 in *Story* features a yellow-haired girl named Pearl whose mother, a desperate widow, offers her child's sexual favors to men to buy food for her family. Not a good story, "Masses of Men" was republished in the collection *Kneel to the Rising Sun* (New York, 1935).

6. Heuermann has categorized them to some extent in the titles of the chapters of his monograph; for example: *"Wege der Adoleszenz," "Kammern des Schreckens," "Geschichten vom begrabenen Leben"* and so forth *(Erskine Caldwells Short Stories).*

7. Unless otherwise noted, all short story references in this chapter are to *The Complete Stories of Erskine Caldwell* (Boston, 1941).

8. Hazel, "Notes on Erskine Caldwell," in *Southern Renascence,* ed. Rubin and Jacobs, p. 316.

9. Erskine Caldwell, *Annette* (New York, 1973), p. 3.

10. Erskine Caldwell, *Tobacco Road* (New York, 1932), p. 223.

11. In later novels, Caldwell sometimes grew excessively careless about dialogue. For example, Rick Sutter, a novelist in *Love and Money* (New York, 1954) says to a cocktail waitress: "I want you to know my friends, Tess. They are real good friends of mine." This novel is one of Caldwell's weakest.

12. Caldwell seems to think of both Jeeter Lester and Ty Ty Walden as biblical patriarchs and clearly identifies Jeeter with Job. Ty Ty's fear that blood will pollute his land reminds us, as James Korges has noted, of God's injunction to Moses in Numbers 35:33.

13. It is probably not a coincidence that West's columnist-protagonist "Miss Lonelyhearts" receives a pathetic letter from a girl "born without a nose" who signs herself "desperate." West was writing *Miss Lonelyhearts* in 1931 while managing the Sutton Hotel where he offered Caldwell a room. Caldwell undoubtedly showed West *Tobacco Road,* then awaiting publication by Scribner's, and West was unconsciously influenced by Sister Bessie Rice.

14. This preoccupation with violence was once considered another bond between Faulkner and Caldwell, writers of the "School of Cruelty" as Henry Seidel Canby called them because their proclivity for mutilation and putrescence seemed greater than that of earlier naturalists. In fairness, we must recall that the stories of both were appearing in great number in a short period of time. Thus, the effect of gratuitous violence was magnified. Shields McIlwaine mentions *As I Lay Dying* (1930) and "The Hound" (1931) as particularly gruesome examples of Faulkner's concern with rotting bodies. ("The Hound" was later published in *The Hamlet.*) "Savannah River Payday" dates from the same year. McIlwaine is careful to point out that emphasis on the violent and squalid aspects of southern life is endemic to southern writers and cities as an early precedent William Byrd who "was amused at the squalor of the North Carolina [?] lubbers."

15. Erskine Caldwell, *The Bastard* (New York, 1929), p. 14.

16. Erskine Caldwell, *Tobacco Road* (New York, 1932), p. 154.

17. Erskine Caldwell, *Georgia Boy* (New York, 1943), p. 205.

18. Ibid., p. 129.

Chapter Seven

1. The condescending tone of the following 1957 *Time* magazine review of *Certain Women* typifies the treatment Caldwell could expect a dozen years after World War II: "This book represents Erskine *(Tobacco Road)* Caldwell's annual defense of a title that is indisputably his—America's No. 1 cracker-barrel pornographer. . . . Since about 40 million hard- and soft-cover copies of his 34 books have been snapped up by U.S. and foreign readers *(God's Little Acre* tops the list with more than 8,000,000 copies sold), the reader can only conclude that to leer is human" *(Time* 70 [Sept. 30, 1957]; 102).

2. Ronald E. Martin, *The Fiction of Joseph Hergesheimer* (Philadelphia, 1965), pp. 251–52.

3. Ibid., p. 251

4. Ibid., p. 250.

5. For a number of the ideas here I am indebted to discussions with Sheldon Grebstein, president of the State University of New York at Purchase.

6. Max Brand, as quoted in *An Informal History of the Pulp Magazine* by Ron Goulard (New York: Ace Books, 1972), p. 134.

7. Frank Luther Mott, *Golden Multitudes* (New York, 1960), p. 290.

8. Ibid.

9. Erskine Caldwell, *Summertime Island* (New York, 1968), p. 146.

Selected Bibliography

PRIMARY SOURCES

Only the most important works are mentioned. No attempt has been made to include uncollected pieces of nonfiction or to list separately the short stories. For a splendidly extensive bibliography of Caldwell's short fiction—chiefly, but not exclusively, the short stories—see Scott MacDonald, "An Evaluative Check-List of Erskine Caldwell's Short Fiction," *Studies in Short Fiction* 15(1978):81–97. Professor MacDonald provides dates and sources of publication for the short stories as well as helpful critical and bibliographical comments. See also his "Erskine Caldwell" in *First Printings of American Authors* (Detroit, 1978).

1. Novels and novellas (listed chronologically)
The Bastard. New York: Heron Press, 1929.
Poor Fool. New York: Rariora Press, 1930.
Tobacco Road. New York: Scribner's Sons, 1932.
God's Little Acre. New York: Viking, 1933.
Journeyman. New York: Viking, 1935.
The Sacrilege of Alan Kent. Portland, Maine: Falmouth Book House, 1936.
Trouble in July. New York: Duell, Sloan & Pearce, 1940.
All Night Long. New York: Duell, Sloan & Pearce, 1942.
Georgia Boy. New York: Duell, Sloan & Pearce, 1943.
Tragic Ground. New York: Duell, Sloan & Pearce, 1944.
A House in the Uplands. New York: Duell, Sloan & Pearce, 1946.
The Sure Hand of God. New York: Duell, Sloan & Pearce, 1947.
This Very Earth. New York: Duell, Sloan & Pearce, 1948.
Place Called Estherville. New York: Duell, Sloan & Pearce, 1949.
Episode in Palmetto. New York: Duell, Sloan & Pearce, 1950.
A Lamp for Nightfall. New York: Duell, Sloan & Pearce, 1952.
Love and Money. New York: Duell, Sloan & Pearce, 1954.
Gretta. Boston: Little, Brown, 1955.
Claudelle Inglish. Boston: Little, Brown, 1958.
Jenny by Nature. New York: Farrar, Straus & Cudahy, 1961.
Close to Home. New York: Farrar, Straus & Cudahy, 1962.
The Last Night of Summer. New York: Farrar, Straus, 1963.
Miss Mamma Aimee. New York: New American Library, 1967.

Summertime Island. New York: World Publishing Co., 1968.
The Weather Shelter. New York: World Publishing Co., 1969.
The Earnshaw Neighborhood. New York: World Publishing Co., 1971.
Annette. New York: New American Library, 1973.

2. Story Collections (listed chronologically)
American Earth. New York: Scribner's Sons, 1931.
We Are the Living. New York: Viking, 1933.
Kneel to the Rising Sun. New York: Viking, 1935.
Southways. New York: Viking, 1938.
Jackpot. New York: Duell, Sloan & Pearce, 1940.
The Complete Stories. Boston: Little, Brown, 1941.
Gulf Coast Stories. Boston: Little, Brown, 1956.
Certain Women. Boston: Little, Brown, 1957.
When You Think of Me. Boston: Little, Brown, 1959.

3. Anthologies (listed chronologically)
Stories by Erskine Caldwell. Edited by Henry Seidel Canby. New York: Somerset Books, 1944.
The Caldwell Caravan: Novels and Stories. Edited by Erskine Caldwell. Cleveland and New York: World Publishing Co., 1946.
The Humorous Side of Erskine Caldwell. Edited by Robert Cantwell. New York: Duell, Sloan & Pearce, 1951.
The Courting of Susie Brown. Introduction by Erskine Caldwell. New York: Duell, Sloan & Pearce, 1952.
Men and Women. Introduction by Carvel Collins. Boston: Little, Brown, 1961.

4. Travel Sketches, Reportage, Criticism, Autobiography, Social Commentary (listed chronologically)
Tenant Farmer. New York: Phalanx Press, 1935.
Some American People. New York: R. M. MacBride, 1935.
All-out on the Road to Smolensk. New York: Duell, Sloan & Pearce, 1942.
Moscow Under Fire. London: Hutchinson, 1942.
Call It Experience. New York: Duell, Sloan & Pearce, 1951.
Around About America. New York: Farrar, Straus, 1964.
In Search of Bisco. New York: Farrar, Straus & Giroux, 1965.
Writing in America. New York: Phaedra, 1968.
Deep South. New York: Weybright & Talley, 1969.
Afternoons in Mid-America. New York: Dodd, Mead & Co., 1976.

5. Photo-Essays with Margaret Bourke-White (listed chronologically)
You Have Seen Their Faces. New York: Viking, 1937.

North of the Danube. New York: Viking, 1939.
Say, Is This the U.S.A. New York: Duell, Sloan & Pearce, 1941.
Russia at War. London and New York: Hutchinson, 1942.

6. Juvenile Literature
Molly Cottontail. Boston: Little, Brown, 1958.
The Deer at Our House. New York: Collier Books, 1966.

7. Recording
"Naturalism in the American Novel." Tape Recording. In *McGraw-Hill*
     Sound Seminars. Tucson, 1950.

SECONDARY SOURCES

Caldwell is mentioned in scores of critical surveys of American literature. I
have therefore listed below only some of the better known or more perspi-
cacious ones. While the number of essays devoted to his work are far fewer,
their numbers are still too great for this bibliography. These tend to have
been written either at the time when he was judged "quite the equal of
Faulkner"—if not his superior—or more recently as part of a "mini" revival
sparked by several academic critics. In addition, his editors Henry Seidel
Canby, Robert Cantwell, and Carvel Collins have written illuminatingly
about him in their introductions. I have ignored most Caldwell interviews
since they are rarely helpful.

1. Complete Books
Heuermann, Hartmut. *Erskine Caldwells Short Stories*. Frankfurt/Main: Pe-
     ter Lang, 1974. Surveys Caldwell's European reputation and attempts
     to place him in an appropriate American tradition; scholarly, thor-
     ough, and helpful. In German, with excellent bibliography.
Korges, James. *Erskine Caldwell*. Pamphlet on American Writers, no. 78.
     Minneapolis: University of Minnesota Press, 1969. Exaggerates Cald-
     well's achievement in a tone sometimes annoyingly ex cathedra; none-
     theless a monograph of great insight.
Sutton, William. *Black Like it Is/Was: Erskine Caldwell's Treatment of Ra-
     cial Themes*. Metuchen, N.J.: Scarecrow Press, 1974. Scattergun treat-
     ment of "racial themes" and potpourri of Caldwellia.

2. Book Excerpts and Articles
Allen, Walter. *The Modern Novel in Britain and the United States*. New
     York: Dutton, 1964, pp. 119–20. A lesser Faulkner but a writer who
     commands respect.

Beach, Joseph Warren. *American Fiction, 1920–1940.* New York: Macmillan Co., 1941, pp. 219–53. An appreciative consideration of Caldwell's methods.

Bode, Carl. "Erskine Caldwell: A Note for the Negative." *College English* 18 (1956):357–59. Calls the later novels "shoddy" and accuses Caldwell of ignoring the changes since the New Deal and World War II. Praises his vitality and assesses Caldwell as a minor writer of some genuine ability.

Bourke-White, Margaret. *Portrait of Myself.* New York: Simon & Schuster, 1963. Devotes a good deal of space to a "fascinating, gifted, difficult man" "whose insecurity" finally acted "as a blind against the world."

Bradbury, John M. *Renaissance in the South.* Chapel Hill: University of North Carolina Press, 1963, pp. 100–101. Denies Caldwell's characters as human beings. Helpful on modern southern literature.

Burke, Kenneth. "Caldwell, Maker of Grotesques." *New Republic* 82 (1935):232–35. Recognizes the strong antirealistic strain in Caldwell's writing and the "balked religiosity" of his best novels.

Cantwell, Robert. "Caldwell's Characters: Why Don't They Leave?" *Georgia Review* 11 (1957):252–64. Discusses the symbolic quality of the landscape in Caldwell's stories, the "psychological consequences" engendered by the depleted soil, and the quandary experienced in attempted flights.

Cargill, Oscar. "Primitivists." In *Intellectual America.* New York: Macmillan, 1941. Defines Caldwell chiefly as a primitivist and a writer of his time influenced by Anderson and Faulkner.

Coindreau, Maurice. *The Time of William Faulkner.* Columbia: University of South Carolina Press, 1971, pp. 113–22. French man of letters admires Caldwell's lyricism and humor but displays grave doubts about *The Bastard.*

Collins, Carvel. "Erskine Caldwell at Work." *Atlantic* 202 (July 1958):21–27. Caldwell interviewed at fifty-four.

Cook, Sylvia Jenkins. *From Tobacco Road to Route 66: The Southern Poor White in Fiction.* Chapel Hill: University of North Carolina Press, 1976. Includes a chapter, "Caldwell's Politics of the Grotesque." Grotesquerie serves Caldwell's essentially pessimistic vision of an exploited class.

Cowley, Malcolm. *—And I Worked at the Writer's Trade.* New York: The Viking Press, 1978, pp. 113–32. A sympathetic retrospection.

⸻ . "The Two Erskine Caldwells." *New Republic* 111 (November 1944):599–600. Caldwell is often contradictory; the storyteller and sociologist are often at odds.

Frohock, Wilbur M. *The Novel of Violence in America, 1920–1950.* Dallas: Southern Methodist University Press, 1957. Caldwell's novels contain a plethora of incompatible elements leaving readers uncertain what attitude to assume toward his work.

Gosset, Louise Y. "The Climate of Violence: Wolfe, Caldwell, Faulkner." In *Violence in Southern Recent Fiction*. Durham, N.C.: Duke University Press, 1965. At his weakest, "horror that is never resolved into pity."

Gray, James. "Local Habitation." In *On Second Thought*. Minneapolis: University of Minnesota Press, 1946. Great praise for Caldwell as social critic.

Gray, R. J. "Southwestern Humor, Erskine Caldwell, and the Comedy of Frustration." *Southern Literary Journal* 8 (Fall 1975):3–26. Discusses Caldwell's humor in terms of the southwestern tradition and recognizes him as an unwitting proponent of Brechtian *Verfremdung*.

Gurko, Leo. *The Angry Decade*. New York: Dodd, Mead & Co., 1947. Praise with many reservations for a writer socially "more progressive" than Faulkner.

Hatcher, H. H. "Proletarian Novel." In *Creating the Modern American Novel*. New York: Farrar & Rinehart, 1935, pp. 273–74. Caldwell very reluctantly lumped with "proletarian" novelists on the basis of his economic concerns.

Hazel, Robert. "Notes on Erskine Caldwell." In *Southern Renascence*. Edited by L. D. Rubin and R. D. Jacobs. Baltimore: John Hopkins Press, 1953. Caldwell is a "southern" writer though he lacks a southern *Sprachgefühl*.

Jacobs, Robert D. "The Humor of Tobacco Road." In *The Comic Imagination in American Literature*. Edited by Louis D. Rubin. New Brunswick, N.J.: Rutgers University Press, 1973. Considers comedy, tragedy, and the alienation effect (or *Verfremdungseffekt*) without using that useful word.

Kirkland, Jack. *Tobacco Road*. In *50 Best Plays of the American Theater*. Edited by Clive Barnes. Introductions by John Gassner. New York: Crown Publishers, 1969. Some great differences from the novel in Broadway's third longest running play.

Krutch, Joseph W. "The Case of Erskine Caldwell." *Nation* 146 (12 February 1938):190. A mixed review of the short-lived dramatization of *Journeyman* in which Caldwell's "creative imagination" is praised.

————. "Tragedy: Eugene O'Neill." In *American Drama Since 1918*. New York: G. Braziller, 1957, pp. 121–28. Not particularly sympathetic treatment of the dramatizations of *Tobacco Road* and *Journeyman*.

Kubie, Lawrence S. "*God's Little Acre:* An Analysis." *Saturday Review of Literature* 19 (1934):306, 307, 312. A psychiatrist considers Freudian currents in *God's Little Acre;* stimulating.

Landor, Mikhail. "Erskine Caldwell in the Soviet Union." *Soviet Literature* 3 (1969):181–86. "Undoubtedly Leftist . . . genuine art."

Loggins, V. "Regional Variations." In *I Hear America*. New York: Thomas Y. Crowell Co., 1937, pp. 221–24. Enthusiastically partisan, relegates Faulkner "to the realm of romance"; Caldwell becomes a "cool-headed realist."

MacDonald, Scott. "Erskine Caldwell 1903—." In *First Printings of American Authors*. Detroit: Gale Research Co., 1978. Valuable bibliographical contribution.

————. "Repetition as Technique in the Short Stories of Erskine Caldwell." *Studies in American Fiction* 5 (Fall 1977):213–25. Turns what some others regard as stylistic liability into asset.

————. "An Evaluative Check-List of Erskine Caldwell's Short Fiction." *Studies in Short Fiction* 15 (1978):81–97. Indispensable, like Heuermann, Korges, and Collins, MacDonald offers titles of stories judged superior.

McIlwaine, Shields. *The Southern Poor-White from Lubberland to Tobacco Road*. Norman: University of Oklahoma Press, 1939. The "lubber" or poor white in southern tradition.

MacLachlan, John M. "Folk and Culture in the Novels of Erskine Caldwell." *Southern Folklore Quarterly* 9 (1945):93–101. Caldwell's picture of the rural southerner is highly inaccurate.

Marion, J. H. Jr. "Star-dust above 'Tobacco Road' ". *Christian Century* 55 (16 February 1938):204–6. Blesses Caldwell, another Zola, for flinging "muck . . . among the magnolias."

Marshall, Margaret. "Caldwell Comes a Cropper." *Nation* 155 (26 December 1942):720. Calls *All Night Long* one of Caldwell's worst; brief review overrates *Trouble in July*, but otherwise quite perceptive.

Owen, Guy. "Erskine Caldwell's Unpublished Poems." *South Atlantic Bulletin* 43 (May 1978):53–57. Writing of poems contributed to Caldwell's artistic development.

————. " 'The Bogus Ones': A Lost Erskine Caldwell Novel." *Southern Literary Journal* 11 (Fall 1978):32–39. Undistinguished early book anticipates later "themes and techniques."

Van Doren, Carl Clinton. *The American Novel, 1789–1939*. New York: Macmillan, 1940, pp. 354–55. Caldwell resembles A. B. Longstreet, "stories seem to descend from an older mode."

Wade, John D. "Sweet Are the Uses of Degeneracy." *Southern Review* 1 (1936):449–66. Literate but defensive against Caldwell's libel of the South.

3. Other Sources Used for the Completion of This Book

Anderson, Maxwell. *Off Broadway*. New York: Bowker, 1960.

Becker, George J., ed. *Documents of Modern Literary Realism*. Princeton, N.J.: Princeton University Press, 1963.

Brecht, Bertolt. *Brecht on Theater*. Translated and edited by John Willet. New York: Hill & Wang, 1964.

Couch, William T., ed. *Culture in the South*. Chapel Hill: University of North Carolina Press, 1935.

Faulkner, William. *The Hamlet*. New York: Random House, 1940.

French, Warren. *The Social Novel at the End of an Era*. Carbondale: South Illinois University Press, 1966.

Hackett, Alice Payne. *Sixty Years of Best Sellers, 1895–1955*. New York: R. R. Bowker Co., 1956.

Hart, James D. *The Popular Book*. New York: Oxford University Press, 1950.

Heggen, Thomas. *Mister Roberts*. Boston: Houghton Mifflin Co., 1946.

Kolb, Harold H. *The Illusion of Life: American Realism as a Literary Form*. Charlottesville: University of Virginia Press, 1969.

Lewis, Oscar. *La Vida*. New York: Random House, 1966.

Lewis, R. W. B. Afterword to *The Confidence Man*, by Herman Melville. New York: New American Library, 1964.

Marcuse, Herbert. *An Essay on Liberation*. Boston: Beacon Press, 1969.

Martin, Ronald E. *The Fiction of Joseph Hergesheimer*. Philadelphia: University of Pennsylvania Press, 1965.

Mott, Frank Luther. *Golden Multitudes*. New York: Bowker, 1960.

Norris, Frank. "Zola as a Romantic Writer." In *The Literary Criticism of Frank Norris*. Edited by Donald Pizer. Austin: University of Texas, 1964.

Nye, Russel. *The Unembarrassed Muse: The Popular Arts in America*. New York: Dial Press, 1970.

Parrington, Vernon L. *Main Currents in American Thought*. New York: Harcourt, Brace & Co., 1926.

Pizer, Donald. *Realism and Naturalism in Nineteenth Century American Literature*. Carbondale: Southern Illinois University Press, 1966.

Reich, Wilhelm. *The Sexual Revolution: Toward a Self-Regulating Character Structure*. Translated by Therese Pol. New York: Farrar, Straus & Giroux, 1974.

Spiller, Robert E., et al. *Literary History of the United States*. Rev. ed. New York: Macmillan Co., 1953.

Tate, Allen. Introduction to *Sanctuary*, by William Faulkner. New York: New American Library, 1968.

Thompson, Stith. *Motif Index of Folk Literature*. Vol. 5. Bloomington: University of Indiana Press, 1955.

Thoreau, Henry David. *The Variorum Walden*. Edited by Walter Harding. New York: Twayne Publishers, 1962.

Tindall, George Brown. *The Emergence of the New South, 1913–1945*. Chapel Hill: Louisiana State University Press, 1967.

Turnbull, Andrew. *Letters of F. Scott Fitzgerald.* New York: Scribner's, 1963.

Wager, Willis. *American Literature: A World View.* New York: New York University Press, 1968.

Walcutt, Charles Child. *American Literary Naturalism, a Divided Stream.* Minneapolis: University of Minnesota Press, 1956.

Index